THE PRAYERS
OF
JOHN OF THE CROSS

THE PRAYERS
OF
JOHN OF THE CROSS

edited and introduced by
Alphonse Ruiz, O.C.D.

New City Press

Published in the United States by New City Press
202 Cardinal Rd., Hyde Park, NY 12538
©1991 New City Press

Introductions and editorial comments translated
by Edward Flood from the original Spanish edition
San Juan de la Cruz—Maestro de la Oración
©1989 Imprenta Monte Carmelo, Burgos, Spain

Cover photo: Anonymous 17th century portrait of John of the Cross,
Valladolid, Spain.

Library of Congress Cataloging-in-Publication Data:

John of the Cross, Saint, 1542-1591.
   [San Juan de la Cruz, maestro de la oración. English]
   The Prayers of Saint John of the Cross / [edited by] Alphonse Ruiz
; [introduction and editorial comments translated by Edward Flood ;
prayers . . . translated by Kieran Kavanaugh and Otilio Rodriguez].

   Translation of: San Juan de la Cruz, maestro de la oración.
   ISBN 1-56548-073-2 : $8.95
   1. Spiritual life—Catholic authors—Early works to 1800.
2. Prayers—Early works to 1800.   I. Ruiz, Alphonse.
II. Kavanaugh, Kieran, 1928- .   III. Rodriguez, Otilio.
IV. Title.
BX2179.J63S2613 1991
248.3—dc20   91-24361

1st printing: October 1991
2d printing: July 1994

Printed in the United States of America

TABLE OF CONTENTS

1. Living Prayer

2. Doctrine on Prayer

1.

Living Prayer

INTRODUCTION

From the testimony of those who at one time or another found Saint John entranced in prayer, it can be easily concluded that prayer was something connatural to him. In fact, prayer was such an intimate and solid experience that it occupied not only part of his time but his whole life and being. Prayer was like his own breathing, something he experienced without effort or a preestablished plan; something that filled his mind and stemmed spontaneously from his heart.

However, should the data of those who knew Saint John more closely be the only testimony we had to evaluate his experience of prayer, our ability to measure it in its true depth would be limited and ultimately reduced to a superficial and purely external appreciation. We would know the different "methods" he used to pray but we would not be able to sense the "substance" of his prayer, those profound and unique tones which characterized his dialogue and relation with God, so absolutely and radically different from that of anyone else, since every creature is, in fact, unique.

Living prayer

Therefore, if we wish to discover the truth underlying the prayer of the saints, the specific and actual weight of their spiritual experience and the tone of their daily dialogue with the Lord, we must resort to no one else but the saints themselves. Only through their words and deep faith can we catch a glimpse of their mysterious encounter and relationship with God. Only by being listeners and living witnesses of their prayer can we grasp their experience and measure their strength.

Can we? - and is this
what we aim for?

Fortunately enough, even today we can learn from the saints' experience by listening in wonder to their inflamed dialogue with God. However, we shall not turn to what witnesses have "heard" about the saints, since such testimony could be disputable, however accurate it may seem to us. Thus, we can go straight to the fountain by enjoying and listening to Saint John's vibrant and everlasting words, which have overflowed his heart despite his prudence and natural modesty. Due to this latter disposition, we believe that had he wished to conceal anything from us, that would have been his intimate dialogue with God. And by reading his books we realize how much care he exercised in silencing every feeling or personal experience that might highlight his own self. Fortunately, however, he has not always been successful in doing so. There are times when the strength of his intimate dialogue with the Lord betrays him, forcing him to give vent to his personal prayer, which springs out irrepressibly from his heart.

These fragments, scattered throughout all his writings, are those we now wish to trace not merely to grasp the width and depth of his personal prayer but to let ourselves be guided and instructed by his experience as a mystagogue. This, of course, does not mean that we must use his words in our own prayer as ready-made formulas that may be found in a prayer book and applied to any circumstance of our lives.

In fact, his prayers do not belong and do not have any sense in a prayer book, nor can they be used indiscriminately since they are extremely personal, shaped within the context of the Saint's own life and work as a writer. Since they follow the thread of his personal reflections and describe his own experience of God, no one but himself could use them to express their personal relationship with God. Of course, we could easily repeat his words but they would never bear the vitality and meaning they had when spoken by Saint John. Such prayers are so precise, so personal in their tone and content, so strongly bearing the impression mark of their author, that they are quite unlikely to accommodate any given purpose. They are more useful in telling us how Saint John prayed than in providing us material for our own prayer, even though they shall always be an incentive and a stimulus to our prayer. In fact, his words may sometimes reflect a feeling or an experience of ours we are not able to express in our own words.

Contradiction

The use of poetry in prayer

The fact that his words sometimes seem to reflect our own experience may happen to us more particularly when reading his poems, which often conceal not only a lyric and loving vibration of words but a fervent prayer as well. In fact, Saint John's poetry is so rich in meaning and mystery, so down to earth and close to those who seek God through their faith, that it will probably never fail to voice our own feelings and experiences. Indeed, he is that poet we all would have wished to be in order to express our personal experiences, which despite having remained locked incommunicado within us, the writer is able to express with great ease and beauty. The prayer enclosed in his writings is somewhat unique but can also reflect our own experiences, our own tormented pilgrimage in the night and our ever unsatisfied longing. This is, perhaps, the most outstanding characteristic of his poetry, never dated despite the relentless passing of time. Thus, any of his poems can help us express our own feelings, since he received the grace and wisdom to adequately express what the rest of us have not even been able to babble.

On the other hand, we must acknowledge that Saint John's poetry is not only a "return to the divine," as he himself describes it, of lyrics and human feelings, but a product of his prayer and intimate encounter with God. Thus, his poetry can be used in prayer and it is in prayer that it finds its best resonance. In fact, perhaps it is only in prayer that we shall be able to experience the real meaning and essence of his lines. And this is independently from the meaning the Saint may have given to his prayers when elaborating on them at a later stage in his major works. Moreover, his poetry is suitable for praying because it is rooted in his own prayer, a fact declared and acknowledged by the Church, who has drawn inspiration from the Saint's lines for the Liturgy of Hours and hymns that are chanted on specific festivities such as Pentecost and the Holy Trinity.

While every stanza stemmed from and was baked in the furnace of Saint John's living prayer, we shall only select from his anthology those lines that recall a personal dialogue with God. In other words, the living dialogue between the human creature and God often consisting in the complaints, yearnings, petitions and expressions of joy addressed to God by those who no longer expect an answer from faith but are contented with enjoying and living in the certainty of his love.

Prayer as a loving dialogue

The same holds true for those fragments we have selected from the Saint's prose. The criteria used in discerning whether we are dealing with prayer and not mere theological reflection have been the following: Since prayer involves an encounter and dialogue with God, every conversational text referring to a *You* or Second Person should be considered prayer. However, that Second Person is not always God himself but a creature made in his likeness, such as our own soul or another human being, who makes this dialogue real. Such exchange expresses the loving relationship between every creature and their Creator, between our soul and God, often reflecting realities that have a typically feminine connotation, such as God's tenderness and protection, and even more importantly, the nuptial union between God and our soul.

Since we are searching for a stimulus for our personal prayer, there are obviously many other texts by Saint John beyond those we have selected, equally stemming from his experience of prayer, which can serve this purpose and help us in our meditation. However, we have only selected those texts that are more expressive, in which his dialogue with God can be perceived, a dialogue that often has the meaning and shape of a vital and personal prayer.

This leads us to another reflection regarding the Saint's prayer. Evidently, the type of prayer we are referring to is much deeper, comprehensive and richer than we thought from the apparently simple fragments we now find scattered throughout his writings. We know, in fact, that when he prayed the psalms and canticles, he had the ability to go beyond their historic context of salvation and interpret the message God wished to convey through them, a message he received as an imperative summons that could not go unanswered. Besides, given the excellence and sensitivity of his spirit, the emotional and colloquial vibration established between him and God must have been an intense and habitual practice, in which the Saint gave full vent to his inner feelings. However, because of his proverbial modesty and self-control, most of his experiences have remained submerged in the silence of his heart.

Circumstantial prayer

In practice, what we know is not enough for us to draw the "measure" of the Saint's spirit of prayer, nor do we have an exact idea of its habitual "tone," since those prayers we are familiar with stem from concrete circumstances, which we would not characterize as everyday situations. Still, a distinction could be drawn between the author's poetic and prosaic prayer. The former is vital, spontaneous prayer, born from a personal and intimate experience that urges the Saint to write about his feelings, whereas the latter stems from his teaching, one of his favorite activities, which included the spiritual guidance he offered to Discalced monks and nuns. So whenever the Saint offered his advice, he knew that there were ears screening his words, a fact that somehow limited his freedom of expression. Moreover, his prayer led to the compelling practice of reflection, which he wished to implant in his Carmelite brothers and sisters. Such reflection had reached maturity first in his personal prayer and was again useful to him in his intimate dialogue with God after putting it in writing. At any rate, even though the Saint's feelings are betrayed through his prosaic prayers, this does not mean the latter are the most personal or natural of his prayers.

The same can be said about his poetry, which he managed to conceal more successfully from his listeners, disciples and witnesses. Logically, we must be satisfied with what we have. And while these prayers were not aimed at teaching or at exhibiting his personal devotion or at being used as a model, it is because of them that we have gained some knowledge about his experience in this field.

Prayer of detachment and wonder

An element that appears almost constantly in Saint John's prayers is that he is free and not governed by self-interest. In other words, his encounter and dialogue with God are not motivated by a necessity or the anxiety of a petition but stems from his loving complacency and the grateful memory of what he has already received from the Lord. Therefore, they are not prayers of request but of gratitude and admiration, as we shall see more in detail in the fragments included in the *Flame*, the warmest and most fervent of his prayers. These all start with an utterance of wonder which sometimes conceals the soul's impatience and suffering for not being able to reach once and for all its union with God, the ultimate cause of its nostalgia and yearning.

Even though Saint John does not say it explicitly, this longing is always at the background of his prayers. It is the implicit theme of all his works and the permanent claim serving as the motivation and reason to justify and demand every dispossession and spiritual night leading to the union of our soul with God. It is a calling often perceived and fulfilled in the loving encounter of prayer.

A more thorough study of the subject and of the personal experience of prayer in the life and writings of the Saint would require many other aspects to be considered. However, since the sole intention of this book is to offer a selection of his prayers and teachings, what we have said suffices as an elementary introduction to the writings we are interested in and which describe his personal experiences.

A classification of Saint John's prayers

Saint John's prayers can be approached in several ways, the simplest of which is to present them exactly as they appear in his writings. Nevertheless, we have decided to assemble them according to certain characteristics which would not exclude, however, other classifications. Thus, we may group his prayers in five large compartments. The first compartment consists of those included in his *Sayings of Light and Love*, with a special emphasis on the prayer of the soul in love, which is certainly unique in its kind. Then there is a section consisting of *soliloquies*, in which the soul speaks to itself, though its thoughts about God are still present in the background. The third group is made up by those prayers that address God directly, which we have called *dialogues*. The fourth selection assembles the prayers of admiration and praise we have already referred to, included in the *Flame*. The fifth and final group consists of brief prayers, also colloquial in genre. The latter are vivid examples of God's personal and familiar response to our soul's supplications.

In order to better understand each type of prayer, we are offering at the beginning of each fragment a reference to the context in which that piece of writing developed, that is to say, the special atmosphere surrounding it, may it be a complaint or a supplication to God. At times, a reference is also added as to the chances we may have of making that prayer ours, according to our own circumstances. In fact, beyond their original motivation these prayers are obviously offered to us today as a stimulus and incentive for our own prayer to God, for which, as experience shows, we do not always find words that are adequate or vital enough.

However, what is important here is not our previous explanation or reference to each context, but those pure, simple, inflamed and loving words addressed by the Saint to the Lord.

SAYINGS OF LIGHT AND LOVE

If we were to make a selection from Saint John's prosaic writings of those that better and more concisely define the depth of his thinking and the sensitivity of his spirit, we would have to choose his brief treatise called *Sayings of Light and Love*. Although this work consists only of a few short pages, it is so overflowing with the love and light borne by its title, so filled with wisdom, that it suffices to offer us an accurate description of their author.

In reality, these pages are not strictly a spiritual treatise since the Saint did not intend to make a systematic exposition of any doctrinal point. They are only a collection of rational, suggestive and well-defined thoughts about the most assorted and vital spiritual matters. However, these writings also have certain characteristics we cannot ignore. In fact, they are not a selection from different sections of his works but were shaped even before his works were compiled. They constitute the core of Saint John's spirituality, which he later developed in more detail in his major works.

These pages also have an extraordinary quality. In fact, before ever belonging to a collection as presented to us today, most of them constituted a personal piece of advice, a gift offered by the Saint to certain individuals who needed some of his light and love as a stimulus for their journey. That means that each saying was inspired at a particular moment and circumstance and was addressed to concrete people, religious men and women who were disciples and followers of the Saint. Each saying contains a beat, an emotional pronouncement of the Saint, whose original liveliness was only perceived by his addressees, though his echo can still be heard by anyone reading his works.

Most probably, without any intention on the part of the writer some of these brief and vigorous sayings have taken the shape of personal prayers filled with intensity and splendor. They are prayers that have stemmed spontaneously from a heart confronted by the doubts or supplications of other people, a heart eager to help and share with others its deepest experiences and emotions. They are unleashed prayers, free from contexts and fitting explanations. We could call them the Saint's purest prayers, stripped from any conditioning factor, which we can make our own more easily precisely because they cannot be situated within any temporal or situational context. They are elementary and simple and do not require our having reached a certain stage in our spiritual journey as other of his prayers do in order to be understood. Thus, we are presenting these prayers in their genuine and simple style without adding anything else except that they belong to the series of *Sayings.*

The first prayer is a special prayer. It consists in the prologue the writer places at the beginning when assembling these scattered "sayings." This first writing masterfully explains the motive guiding the Saint in collecting these fragments, that is, his desire to help the others. At the same time, he expresses his fear of losing the treasure of divine wisdom bestowed upon him by God and which he humbly believes he is misusing. The prologue ends with a beautiful supplication containing the writer's profound conviction, which underlies every prayer, that "without the Lord, nothing can be done."

1.

O my God and my delight, for Your love I have also desired to give my soul to composing these sayings of light and love concerning You. Since, although I can express them in words, I do not have the works and virtues they imply (which is what pleases You more, O my Lord, than the words and wisdom they contain), may others, perhaps, moved by them, go forward in Your service and love—in which I am lacking. I will thereby find consolation, that these sayings prove an occasion that what I lack may be found in others.

Lord, You love discretion, You love light, You love love, these three You love above the other operations of the soul. Hence these will be sayings of discretion for the wayfarer, of light for the way, and of love in the long-winded and dry eloquence of weak and artificial human wisdom, sweetness and love, which do indeed please You, removing obstacles and stumbling blocks from the paths of many souls who unknowingly trip and unconsciously walk in the path of error—poor souls who think they are right in what concerns the following of Your Beloved Son, our Lord Jesus Christ, and becoming like Him, imitating His life, actions, and virtues, and the form of His nakedness and purity of spirit. Father of mercies, come to our aid, for without You, Lord, we can do nothing.

(Sayings, Prologue)

2.

O Lord, My God, who will seek You with simple and pure love and not find You are all he desires, for You show Yourself first and go out to meet those who desire You?

(Sayings, 2)

3.

O sweetest love of God, so little known, he who has found its veins is at rest!

(Sayings, 16)

4.

A soul that is hard because of its self-love grows harder. O good Jesus, if You do not soften it, it will ever continue in its natural hardness.

(Sayings, 28)

5.

I didn't know You, my Lord, because I still desired to know and relish things.

(Sayings, 30)

6.

My spirit has become dry because it forgets to feed on You.

(Sayings, 36)

7.

Well and good if all things change, Lord God, provided we are rooted in You.

(Sayings, 31)

8.

Lord, You return gladly and lovingly to lift up the one who offends You and I do not turn to raise and honor him who annoys me.

(Sayings, 44)

9.

O mighty Lord, if a spark from the empire of Your justice effects so much in the mortal ruler who governs the nations, what will Your all-powerful justice do with the righteous and the sinner?

(Sayings, 45)

10.

Lord, my God, You are not a stranger to him who does not estrange himself from You. How do they say that it is You who absent Yourself?

(Sayings, 47)

11.

Going everywhere, my God, with You, everywhere things will happen as I desire for You.

(Sayings, 50)

12.

All for You and nothing for me.

(Maxims, 32)

13.

Oh, how sweet Your presence will be to me, You Who are the supreme good! I must draw near You in silence and uncover my feet before You that You may be pleased to unite me to you in marriage (Ru. 3:7), and I will not rest until I rejoice in Your arms. Now I ask You, Lord, not to abandon me at any time in my recollection, for I am a squanderer of my soul.

(Maxims, 45)

14.

My Beloved, all that is rugged and toilsome I desire for myself, and all that is sweet and delightful I desire for You.

(Maxims, 52)

15.

Oh, how kind our God is!

(Suggestions, 4)

16.
Prayer of the Enraptured Soul

Enclosed in number 26 of Saint John's original version of Sayings *of Light and Love, the prayer of the soul in love is undoubtedly a precious and unique pearl among all his writings. Literally speaking, it is probably the most beautiful prayer of his prose, the most* lively and vibrant piece of his writing, where he has best pictured himself, revealing those personal feelings his natural modesty fails to control. Saint John could have never expressed himself in that manner, revealing his feelings so openly before God, had he not experienced the certainty of God's love, that love he had relished a thousand times before and overflowed in his heart. Never before had he been so spontaneous and effusive.

Even though we shall later come across other prayers full of intensity and emotion echoing the loving fire that burned in his heart, the prayer of the soul in love shall always be an excellent piece of his literary production. This fragment is qualified as a living prayer from beginning to end and is compared to a unique and precious stone among the gems of his works.

Furthermore, the prayer of the enraptured soul offers us a model of what every Christian entreaty should be since it contains three characteristic perceptions that should dwell in any praying heart:

— the awareness of our own poverty and unworthiness, for which our trust should only be placed on the mercy of him who calls us through his grace.

— the certainty that God will listen to us because he who prays in us is Christ, whom God has given each of us as a mediator.

— our gratitude for having been lavished and glorified by God, whom we can love in our heart without hesitation or without having to look for some other gift.

Thus, there is no better piece in Saint John's work to make our own than this prayer, which stems from the sorrowful acknowledgment of our own sins and weaknesses, provided our souls are already inflamed with love. Still, even if they were tepid but wished to be afire, we may hope to be dragged by the force of the Saint's words to an enraptured state. This prayer says:

Lord God, my Beloved, if You remember still my sins in suchwise that you do not do what I beg of You, do Your will concerning them, my God, which is what I most desire, and exercise Your goodness and mercy, and You will be known through them. And if it is that You are waiting for my good works so as to hear my prayer through their means, grant them to me, and work them for me, and the sufferings You desire to accept, and let it be done. But if You are not waiting for my works, what is it that makes You wait, my most clement Lord? Why do You delay? For if, after all, I am to receive the grace and mercy which I entreat of You in Your Son, take my mite, since You desire it, and grant me this blessing, since You also desire that.

Who can free himself from lowly manners and limitations if you do not lift him to Yourself, my God, in purity of love? How will a man begotten and nurtured in lowliness rise up to You, Lord, if You do not raise him with Your hand which made Him?

You will not take from me, my God, what You once gave me in Your only Son, Jesus Christ, in Whom You gave me all I desire. Hence I rejoice that if I wait for You, You will not delay.

With what procrastinations do you wait, since from this very moment you can love God in your heart?

Mine are the heavens and mine is the earth. Mine are the nations, the just are mine, and mine the sinners. The angels are mine, and the Mother of God, and all things are mine; and God Himself is mine and for me, because Christ is mine and all for me.

What do you ask, then, and seek, my soul? Yours is all of this, and all is for you. Do not engage yourself in something less, nor pay heed to the crumbs which fall from your Father's table. Go forth and exult in your Glory! Hide yourself in it and rejoice, and you will obtain the supplications of your heart.

SOLILOQUIES

While every prayer is a dialogue, a communicative encounter with God supported by our faith, it often becomes a monologue or soliloquy due to our faith in the presence of God and his word. In that soliloquy those that are affected by the absence or silence of God can only talk to themselves, while suffering and awaiting God's response.

Nevertheless, God is always close to the soul that longs for him and he fills it with his blessings. Still, the soul is wounded by the feeling of God's absence and thus resorts to a soliloquy in search of consolation. As a matter of fact, the Saint's *Spiritual Canticle* opens precisely with this complaint to God for his absence. And since this protest does not obtain the immediate response it desires, the soul recites a series of soliloquies to console itself, trying to find reasons for God's silence. We may find the soul's unburdening of its troubles in the first song useful to us, who so often experience that same difficulty in encountering God. Thus, we shall convince ourselves of his nearness, as well as of the permanent need to search him through our faith in our own heart, where he can be found more easily.

17.

Oh, then, soul, most beautiful among all the creatures, so anxious to know the dwelling place of your Beloved that you may go in quest of Him and be united with Him, now we are telling you that you yourself are His dwelling and His secret chamber and hiding place. This is something of immense gladness for you, to see that all your good and hope is so close to you as to be within you, or better, that you cannot be without Him.

(*Canticle*, 1:7)

18.

What more do you want, O soul! And what else do you search for outside, when within yourself you possess your riches, delights, satisfactions, fullness, and kingdom—your Beloved whom you desire and seek? Be joyful and gladdened in your interior recollection with Him, for you have Him so close to you. Desire Him there, adore Him there. Do not go in pursuit of Him outside yourself. You will only become distracted and wearied thereby, and you shall not find Him, or enjoy Him more securely, or sooner, or more intimately than by seeking Him within you. There is but one difficulty: Even though He does abide within you, He is hidden. Nevertheless, it is vital for you to know the place of His hiding that you may search for Him there with assuredness. And this, soul, is also what you ask, when with the affection of love you question: "Where have You hidden . . . ?"

(*Canticle*, 1:8)

19.

Yet you inquire: Since He Whom my soul loves is within me, why don't I find Him or experience Him?

The reason is that he remains concealed and you do not also conceal yourself in order to encounter and experience Him. Anyone who is to find a hidden treasure must enter the hiding place secretly, and once he has discovered it, he will also be hidden just as the treasure is hidden. Since, then, your beloved Bridegroom is the treasure hidden in a field, for which the wise merchant sold all his possessions (Mt 13:44), and that field is your soul, in order to find Him you should forget all your possessions and all creatures and hide in the interior, secret chamber of your spirit. And there, closing the door behind you (your will to all things), you should pray to your Father in secret (Mt 6:6). Remaining hidden with Him, you will experience Him in hiding, and love and enjoy Him in hiding, and you will delight with Him in hiding, that is, in a way transcending all language and feeling.

(Canticle, 1:9)

20.

Come, then, O beautiful soul! Since you know now that your desired Beloved lives hidden within your heart, strive to be really hidden with Him, and you will embrace Him within you and experience Him with loving affection. Note that through Isaiah He calls you to this secret chamber: *Come enter into your secret chambers, shut the door behind you* (your faculties to all creatures), *hide yourself a little, even for a moment* (Is 26:20), for this moment of life on earth. If, O soul, in this short space of time you keep diligent watch over your heart, as the Wise Man advises (Prv 4:23), God will undoubtedly give you what He also promises further on through Isaiah: *I shall give you hidden treasures and reveal to you the substance and mysteries of secrets* (Is 45:3).

(Canticle, 1:10)

21.

You have been told, O soul, of the conduct you should observe if you want to find the Bridegroom in your hiding place. Still, if you want to hear this again, listen to a word abounding in substance and inaccessible truth: seek Him in faith and love, without desire for the satisfaction, taste, or understanding of any other thing than what you ought to know. Faith and love are like the blind man's guides. They will lead you along a path unknown to you, to the place where God is hidden.

(Canticle, 1:11)

22.

You do very well, O soul, to seek Him ever as the one hidden, for you exalt God immensely and approach very near Him when you consider Him higher and deeper than anything you can reach. Hence, pay no attention, neither partially nor entirely, to anything which your faculties can grasp. I mean that you should never desire satisfaction in what you understand about God, but in what you do not understand about Him. Never stop with loving and delighting in your understanding and experience God, but love and delight in what is neither understandable nor perceptible of Him. Such is the way, as we said, of seeking Him in faith. However surely it may seem that you find, experience, and understand God, you must, because He is inaccessible and concealed, always regard Him as hidden, and serve Him Who is hidden in a secret way. Do not be like the many foolish ones who, in their lowly understanding of God, think that when they do not understand, taste, or experience Him, He is far away and utterly concealed. The contrary belief would be truer. The less distinct is their understanding of Him, the closer they approach Him, since in the words of the prophet David, *He made darkness His hiding place* (Ps 17:12). Thus in drawing near Him, you will experience darkness because of the weakness of your eye.

You do well, then, at all times, in both adversity and prosperity, whether spiritual or temporal, to consider God as hidden, and call after Him thus: *Where have you hidden, Beloved and left me moaning?*

(Canticle, 1:12)

23.

However, in spite of all the reasons cited to convince itself of God's proximity, the soul is not capable of controlling the grief it feels for his apparent absence, and amazed at the fact that such pain does not utterly destroy it, it turns once more to its soliloquies in the eighth song of the same Canticle:

Life of my soul, how can you endure in this bodily life, for it is death to you and a privation of that true spiritual life of God, in which through essence, love, and desire you live more truly than in the body? And now that this understanding of God's grandeur has not caused you to go out and be freed from the body of this death (Rom 7:24) so as to live and enjoy the life of your God, how can you still live in a body so fragile? Moreover, the wounds of love which you receive from the grandeurs of the Beloved communicated to you are, in themselves alone, enough to end your life. For all of them leave you wounded with vehement love. And the things you experience and understand of Him are as numerous as the touches and wounds you receive of a love that slays.

(*Canticle*, 8:2)

24.

And shortly after, with a lingering feeling of wonder, the soul asks itself:

Moreover, how can you endure in the body, since the touches of love (indicated by the arrows) which the Beloved causes in your heart are enough to take away your life?

(*Canticle*, 8:4)

25.

This recourse also appears in the commentary to the second song of the book of Flame, *where the soul recalls all it has received through God's love, to make that union feasible. It is a love full of gifts and magnificence, befitting he who is the omnipotent and owner of everything. This prayer helps us acknowledge with gratitude how much God has enriched each of us personally and how easily we forget him. It refers, in short, to our lack of correspondence:*

When one loves and does good to another, he loves and does good to him in the measure of his own nature and properties. Thus your Bridegroom, dwelling within you, grants you favors according to His nature. Since He is omnipotent, He omnipotently loves and does good to you; since He is wise, you feel that He loves and does good to you with wisdom; since He is infinitely good, you feel that He loves you with goodness; since He is holy, you feel that with holiness He loves and favors you; since He is just, you feel that in justice He loves and favors you; since He is merciful, mild, and clement, you feel His mercy, mildness, and clemency; since He is a strong, sublime, and delicate being, you feel that His love for you is strong, sublime, and delicate; since He is pure and undefiled, you feel that He loves you in a pure and undefiled way; since He is truth, you feel that He loves you in truthfulness; since He is liberal, you feel that he liberally loves and favors you, without any personal profit, only in order to do good to you; since He is the virtue of supreme humility, He loves you with supreme humility and esteem and makes you His equal, gladly revealing Himself to you in these ways of knowledge, in this His countenance filled with graces, and telling you in this His union, not without great rejoicing: "I am yours and for you and delighted to be what I am so as to be yours and give myself to you."

(Flame, 3:6)

26.

Finally, there is a consoling soliloquy in the second book of the Night. *Referring to the passive purification of our soul the Saint attempts to demonstrate, in connection with the second song of the poem, how the soul is secure even if it travels in darkness. And half-way in his reflection he inserts this prayer, which is an invitation to accept that purification. A prayer we can make perfectly ours every time we feel lost in the nights we must sustain to be purified.*

Oh, then, spiritual soul, when you see your appetites darkened, your inclinations dry and constrained, your faculties incapacitated for any interior exercise, do not be afflicted; think of this as a grace, since God is freeing you from yourself and taking from you your own activity. However well your actions may have succeeded you did not work so completely, perfectly, and securely—owing to their impurity and awkwardness—as you do now that God takes you by the hand and guides you in darkness, as though you were blind, along a way and to a place you know not. You would never have succeeded in reaching this place no matter how good your eyes and your feet.

(2 Night, 16:7)

27.

In addition to these intense and peaceful prayers in which the soul speaks to itself and that are applicable to any soul, the Saint has also written about the intuitively perceived feeling of God's nearness, of which this and the following are only a few fragments:

Happy is the soul who in this life merits at some time the enjoyment of the fragrance of these divine flowers!

(Canticle, 24:6)

28.

Oh, who can tell how impossible it is for a man with appetites to judge the things of God as they are!

(Flame, 3:73)

29.

Oh what a sheer grace it is for the soul to be freed from the house of its senses! This fortune, in my opinion, can only be understood by the man who has savored it.

(2 Night, 14:3)

DIALOGUES

In reality, the monologue or soliloquy may still fall short of being authentic prayer. In fact, while talking to ourselves, even if the thought and image of God are in the background, we may actually be finding a shelter in ourselves, listening and reasoning with ourselves. Thus, it becomes imperative rather than convenient, to converse with Someone, someone different from ourselves. Only in that exchange of words, which is also an exchange of feelings and experiences, shall true prayer stem and forge itself. By talking to him we are saying we believe in his near presence and his acceptance of us, however imperceptible this may appear to our senses. Moreover, by listening to and translating his word into practice we are already proclaiming his love for us. In fact, it is from our listening and conversing in prayer that our friendship with God develops.

Logically, those whose prayers are based upon their faith do not always perceive God's presence and at times must content themselves without his answer. However, they know that this does not imply an absence of dialogue since God also expresses himself in silence.

Eventually, the most important thing, that is our encounter with God, our friend and companion, will take place, provided we come out of ourselves and place our feelings and words in his hands. Thus, only the certainty of his invisible and yet real company will deliver us from the narrow circle of our ego and introduce us to actual prayer, enabling us to move naturally from soliloquy to colloquy, from monologue to dialogue.

It is then that we experience colloquial prayer. It is then that we unburden our soul by addressing God directly, examples of which, as we shall see, abound in the Saint's writings. We shall first examine those that appear in his poems. Among them, we should particularly mention the poem of the *Spiritual Canticle*, which is a prayer in its entirety, a living, ardent dialogue between the soul, the creatures and God himself. Each stanza is an inflamed prayer bearing a meaning of its own. In the first thirteen stanzas the soul moans in its search for God. We shall consider those that are directly addressed to God, whose absence the soul suffers. These can be easily made our own since we are all searchers and pilgrims in the same faith and often experience the distressful feeling of God's absence.

30.

Where have You hidden,
Beloved, and left me moaning?
You fled like the stag
After wounding me;
I went out calling You, and You were gone.

31.

Ah, who has the power to heal me?
Now wholly surrender yourself!
Do not send me
Any more messengers,
They cannot tell me what I must hear.

32.

All who are free
Tell me a thousand graceful things of You;
All wound me more
And leave me dying
Of, ah, I-don't-know-what behind their stammering.

33.

How do you endure
O life, not living where you live?
And being brought near death
By arrows you receive
From that which you conceive of your Beloved.

34.

Why, since You wounded
This heart, don't You heal it?
And why, since You stole it from me,
Do You leave it so,
And fail to carry off what You have stolen?

35.

Extinguish these miseries,
Since no one else can stamp them out;
And may my eyes behold You,
Because You are their light,
And I would open them to You alone.

36.

Show me your presence
that I may die at the sight of your beauty,
since the pain of love can only be healed
by the presence and sight of the beloved.

37.

Withdraw them, Beloved,
I am taking flight!

38.

Still dissatisfied for not having had an answer from God, the soul also talks to God's creatures, addressing them with equally passionate yearning. The actual words Saint John uses in that prayer could serve as a model for that open dialogue with nature, which a more sensitized humankind is more likely to engage in today:

Shepherds, you that go
Up through the sheepfolds to the hill,
If by chance you see
Him I love most,
Tell Him that I sicken, suffer, and die.

39.

O woods and thickets
Planted by the hand of my Beloved!
O green meadow,

Coated, bright, with flowers,
Tell me, has He passed by you?

40.

O spring like crystal!
If only, on your silvered-over face,
You would suddenly form
The eyes I have desired,
Which I bear sketched deep within my heart.

41.

My Beloved is the mountains,
And lonely wooded valleys,
Strange islands,
And resounding rivers,
The whistling of love-stirring breezes,
The tranquil night
At the time of the rising dawn,
Silent music,
Sounding solitude,
The supper that refreshes, and deepens love.

42.

Be still, deadening north wind;
South wind come, you that waken love,
Breathe through my garden,
Let its fragrance flow,
And the Beloved will feed amid the flowers.

43.

Later on, the soul readdresses its Beloved, recalling with deep nostalgia the gifts it savored in that brief encounter it was allowed to have while still on earth and ends its prayer by longing to reach the fulfillment of God's promise.
These stanzas adequately express our gratitude for the graces we

have received through other believers, which we can apply to our
own prayer while travelling toward our final destiny.

With flowers and emeralds
Chosen on cool mornings
We shall weave garlands
Flowering in Your love,
And bound with one hair of mine.
You considered
That one hair fluttering at my neck;
You gazed at it upon my neck
And it captivated You;
And one of my eyes wounded You.

44.

When You looked at me
Your eyes imprinted Your grace in me;
For this You loved me ardently;
And thus my eyes deserved
To adore what they beheld in You.

45.

Do not despise me;
For if, before, You found me dark,
Now truly You can look at me
Since You have looked
And left in me grace and beauty.

46.

Let us rejoice, Beloved,
And let us go forth to behold ourselves in Your beauty,
To the mountain and to the hill,
To where the pure water flows,
And further, deep into the thicket.

47.

And then we will go on
To the high caverns in the rock
Which are so well concealed;
There we shall enter
And taste the fresh juice of the pomegranates.

48.

There You will show me
What my soul has been seeking,
And then You will give me,
You, my Life, will give me there
What You gave me on that other day.

49.

*Saint John wrote other prayers in the form of colloquial poems,
in which the soul complains to God for his apparent absence. Such
are the stanzas of "I live while no longer living in myself" in which
the soul addresses God as follows:*

This life that I live
Is no life at all,
And so I die continually
Until I live with You;
Hear me, my God:
I do not desire this life,
I am dying because I do not die.

50.

When I am not with You
What life can I have
Except to endure
The bitterest death known?
I pity myself
For I go on and on living,
Dying because I do not die.

51.

When I try to find relief
Beholding You in the Sacrament
I find this greater sorrow:
I cannot enjoy You wholly.
All things are affliction
Since I do not see You as I desire,
And I die because I do not die.

52.

And if I rejoice, Lord,
In the hope of seeing You,
Yet seeing I can lose You
Doubles my sorrow.
Living in such fear
And hoping as I hope,
I die because I do not die.

53.

Lift me from this death,
My God, and give me life;
Do not hold me bound
With these so strong bonds;
See how I long to see You;
I am so wholly miserable
That I die because I do not die.

54.

I will cry out for death
And mourn my living
While I am held here
For my sins.
O my God, when will it be
That I can truly say:
Now I live because I do not die?

55.

The poem of the Night *is, on the other hand, more similar to a soliloquy in which at daybreak the soul joyfully remembers the fears and anguishes of its search in the night, to which it sings in love. Also, aware of the importance of faith in leading us to the encounter with God, our soul prays even though it may have not arrived yet at the bright hour of dawn.*

On that glad night,
By the secret, for no one saw me,
Nor did I look at anything,
With no other light or guide
Than the one that burned in my heart.

56.

If there is one poem, however, that condenses the longing of an enraptured soul, caught between the joys already savored and the impatience for a permanent encounter, it is that of the Flame. *The whole poem is a passionate dialogue between the soul and its God, who appears personified in the living flame wrapping and consuming the soul with its fire, while the soul aflame experiences its love for God rekindled.*

According to the author, it is not a prayer that anyone can use as their own, especially if they are not experiencing the same reality as the Saint. Still, no one could recite it as their own even if it expressed the common uneasiness due to the limitations of human life.

How gently and lovingly
You wake in my heart,
Where in secret You dwell alone;
And by Your sweet breathing,
Filled with good and glory,
How tenderly You swell my heart with love!

57.

Naturally, Saint John's prosaic prayers have a different tone from that of his poetic prayers, which does not mean the former are less emotional or loving. Sometimes, the author's dialogues are simply directed to God, as we shall see in the following two fragments. The first is taken from the second book of the Night, *where in reference to the degrees of love of the soul which is not supposed to search God's gifts for its own pleasure, he writes this sensitive and beautiful prayer:*

Ah, my Lord and my God! How many go to You looking for their own consolation and gratification and desiring that You grant them favors and gifts, but those wanting to give You pleasure and something at a cost to themselves, setting aside their own interests, are few. What is lacking is not that You, O my God, desire to grant us favors again, but that we make use of them for Your service alone and thus oblige You to grant them to us continually.

(*2 Night*, 19:4)

58.

The second prayer is taken from the commentary to the fourth stanza in the Flame. *In reference to how every good in us comes from God, who reminds us of our duty to love him, the Saint exclaims:*

Awaken and enlighten us, my Lord, that we might know and love the blessings which You ever propose to us, and that we might understand that You have moved to bestow favors on us and have remembered us.

(*Flame*, 4:9)

59.

In his Ascent of Mount Carmel, *there is a prayer in chapter 38 that describes how those places devoted to prayer should be in order to fulfil God's wishes:*

How many festivals, my God, do the children of men celebrate in Your honor in which the devil has a greater role than You! And the devil, like a merchant, is pleased with these gatherings because he does more business on those days. How many times will You say of them: *This people honors Me with their lips alone, but their*

heart is far from Me, because they serve Me without cause (Mt
15:8-9).

(3 *Ascent*, 38:3)

60.

*Even before, in chapter 31 of the same third book, when referring
to the damage the soul may suffer by becoming attached to God's
gifts, and more specifically to those who may have established a
pact with the devil and may have gone as far as desecrating the
eucharist in order to obtain those gifts, he magnificently expresses
both his awe and trust in God's kindness:*

May God extend and show forth His infinite mercy in this matter!

(3 *Ascent*, 31:5)

61.

On other instances, such as in stanza 13 of the Spiritual Canticle,
the author affectionately calls God his Beloved:

"Withdraw them, Beloved," that is, these Your divine eyes, "for
they cause me to take flight and go out of myself to supreme
contemplation, which is beyond what the sensory part can endure."

(*Canticle*, 13:2)

62.

And in stanza 19 the soul addresses God as follows:

But Beloved, first turn to the interior of my soul, and be enamored
of the company—the riches—You have placed there, so that loving
the soul through them You may dwell and hide in her. For, indeed,
even though they are Yours, since you gave them to her, they also
belong to her . . . going with her through strange islands.

(*Canticle*, 19:6, 7)

63.

The following brief prayer, similar to a sigh or supplication, appears in the commentary to verse 28 in the Canticle *and can be easily applied to each of us since it expresses a longing rather than an experience:*

My Beloved, all that is rough and toilsome I desire for Your sake, and all that is sweet and pleasant I desire for Your sake.

(Canticle, 28:10)

64.

When conversing with God, the writer usually refers to him as "Spouse." It seems that by calling him its Spouse the soul wishes to remind the Lord of his commitment of mutual and indebted love, and itself of its right to hope for the fulfillment of its request. Thus, in the commentary to the first verse of the Canticle *in which the soul expresses its grief for God's absence, we read the following:*

My Spouse, in that touch and wound of Your love, You have not only drawn my soul away from all things, but have also made it go out from self—indeed, it even seems that You draw it out of the body—and You have raised it up to Yourself, while it was calling after You, now totally detached so as to be attached to You.

"And you were gone."

(Canticle, 1:20)

65.

In reference to stanza 6 of the Canticle *and after begging God not to send messengers on his behalf but rather come himself to heal the soul's wound, the writer addresses the following two beautiful prayers to the Spouse:*

Do not let my knowledge of You, communicated through these messengers of news and sentiments about You, any longer be so measured, so remote and alien to what my soul desires. How well You know, my Spouse, that messengers redouble the sorrow of one who grieves over Your absence: first, through knowledge they enlarge the wound; second, they seem to postpone Your coming. From now on do not send me this remote knowledge. If up to this time I could be content with it, because I did not have much knowledge or love of You, now the intensity of my love cannot be satisfied with these messages; therefore: "Now wholly surrender Yourself!"

(Canticle, 6:6)

66.

My Lord, my Spouse, You have given Yourself to me partially; now may You give me Yourself more completely. You have revealed Yourself to me as through fissures in a rock; now may You give me that revelation more clearly. You have communicated by means of others, as if joking with me; now may You truly grant me a communication of Yourself by Yourself. In Your visits, at times, it seems You are about to give me the jewel of possessing You; but when I become aware of this possession, I discover that I do not have it, for You hide this jewel as if you had given it jokingly. Now wholly surrender Yourself by giving Yourself entirely to all of me, that my entire soul may have complete possession of You.
Do not send me
Any more messengers,
They cannot tell me what I must hear.

(Canticle, 6:6)

67.

Later on, in the comment to the words "Hide Yourself, my Love" in verse 19, the soul says:

My dear Spouse, withdraw to the innermost part of my soul and communicate in secret, manifest Your hidden wonders, alien to every mortal eye.

(Canticle, 19:3)

68.

Moreover, this supplication becomes a model of deep prayer:

Let Your divinity shine on my intellect by giving it divine knowledge, and on my will by imparting to it the divine love, and on my memory with the divine possession of glory.

(Canticle 19, 4)

69.

In the commentary to stanza 32, acknowledging God has given it all it possesses, the soul confesses with loving gratitude:

My faculties, the eyes through which I can see You, my Spouse, have merited this elevation which enables them to look at You.

(Canticle, 32:8)

70.

In the commentary to stanza 38 of the Canticle, *the soul resorts to the intimate appellative of "my Spouse" when it prays to God reminding him of its longing for that plenitude which so far it has only been able to sample:*

What You gave me (that weight of glory to which You predestined me, O my Spouse, on the day of Your eternity when you considered it good to decree my creation), You will give me then on the day of my espousals and nuptials and on my day of gladness of heart (Ct 3:11), when loosed from the flesh and within the high caverns of Your chamber, gloriously transformed in You, I shall drink with You the juice of the sweet pomegranates.

(Canticle, 38:9)

71.

On two other instances, the author joins the concept of "Spouse" to that of "Word." Thus, in the commentary to the fourth song in the Flame, *when thanking God for having fulfilled its aspiration to love him, the author exclaims:*

How gentle and loving (that is, extremely loving and gentle) is Your awakening, O Word, Spouse, in the center and depth of my soul, which is its pure and intimate substance, in which secretly and silently, as its only lord, You dwell alone, not only as in Your house, nor only as in Your bed, but also as in my own heart, intimately and closely united to it. And how delicately You captivate me and arouse my affections toward You in the sweet breathing You produce in this awakening, a breathing delightful to me and full of good and glory.

How gently and lovingly You wake in my heart.

(Flame, 4:3, 4)

72.

And upon experiencing God's absence, Saint John writes this brief and loving supplication in the commentary to the first stanza of his Canticle:

O Word, my Spouse, show me where You are hidden.

(Canticle, 1:3)

73.

In addition to these loving dialogues where God is clearly mentioned, however, there are other fragments where his name is not explicitly mentioned, even though the soul is clearly addressing him. Thus, in the commentary to the first stanza of the Canticle, *the soul refers to God's absence:*

At the time I desire to hold fast to Your presence, I did not find You, and the detachment from one without attachment to the other left me suspended in air and suffering, without any support from You or from myself.

(Canticle, 1:21)

74.

In stanza 6, the soul urges God to make his presence felt again and not be contented with sending his messengers. Anyone can make this beautiful confession their own when faced with the same feeling of absence:

I desire complete knowledge of You, and they have neither knowledge nor ability to tell of You entirely. Nothing in heaven or on earth can give the soul the knowledge she desires of You. Thus, "they cannot tell me what I must hear." Instead of these other messengers, may You, then, be both the messenger and message.

(Canticle, 6:7)

75.

In the seventh song, the author insists on the same subject of the messengers' ineptness in showing God to the wounded soul:

Beside the fact that these creatures wound me with the thousand graceful things they explain about You, there is a certain "I-don't-know-what" which one feels is yet to be said, something unknown still to be spoken, and a sublime trace of God, as yet uninvestigated, revealed to the soul, a lofty understanding of God which cannot be put into words. Hence she calls this something "I-don't-know-what." If what I understand wounds me with love, this which I do not understand completely, yet have sublime experience of, is death to me.

(Canticle, 7:9)

76.

And in the commentary to song 9 the author makes the following complaints to God, urging him to complete the work of love he has initiated in his soul:

Why, since You wounded this heart until it has become sorely wounded, do You not heal it by wholly slaying it with love? Since You cause the sore wound in the sickness of love, may You cause health in the death of love. As a result, the heart, wounded with the sorrow of Your absence, will be healed with the delight and glory of Your sweet presence.

(Canticle, 9:3)

77.

Why do You fail to carry off the heart You have stolen through love; and why do You fail to fill, satisfy, accompany, and heal it, giving it complete stability and repose in You?

(Canticle, 9:7)

78.

The commentary to stanza 11 presents a chancy and determined supplication in which the soul bets on death as long as it may be able to enjoy the encounter with its beloved God. This fragment is certainly not within the reach of our faith but that should not prevent us from acknowledging its beauty:

Since the delight arising from the sight of Your being and beauty is unendurable, and since I must die in seeing You, may the vision of Your beauty be my death.

(Canticle, 11:6)

79.

From the entire Canticle, *the commentary to stanza 19 seems to be the most colloquial verse, a living expression of the soul to its Lord and Spouse. This and the following are two further samples of a humble and sincere supplication containing a deeper and more intimate communication with God:*

Do not speak as before when the communications You granted me were such that You spoke them to the exterior senses; that is, You spoke things apprehensible to the senses, since these things were not so high and deep that the sensory part could not attain to them. But now let these communications be so lofty and substantial and interior that You do not speak of them to the senses, that is, such that the senses may be unable to attain to the knowledge of them.

(Canticle, 19:5)

80.

Since I go to You through a spiritual knowledge strange and foreign to the senses, let Your communication be so interior and sublime as to be foreign to all of them.

(*Canticle*, 19:7)

81.

Although the concept of the spouse in the Song of Songs permeates Saint John's entire Spiritual Canticle, *sometimes this fact is more evident and textually quoted. In fact, in stanza 22, in what seems to echo the biblical words, the soul prays boldly to its God:*

You dried up and subdued in me the appetites and passions which in our flesh are the breasts and milk of mother Eve, and an impediment to this state. And when this is accomplished "that I may find you alone outside," that is, outside of all things and of myself, in solitude and nakedness of spirit, which is attained when the appetites are dried up. And alone there, "kiss you" alone, that is, that my nature now alone and denuded of all temporal, natural, and spiritual impurity may be united with You alone, with Your nature alone, through no intermediary.

(*Canticle*, 22:7)

82.

The same thing can be found in stanza 26, in a reference to the wine of wisdom the soul wishes to receive from the Beloved.

There You will teach me (wisdom and knowledge and love), *and I shall give You a drink of spiced wine* (my love spiced with Yours, transformed in Yours) (Ct 8:2).

(*Canticle*, 26:6)

83.

The Spiritual Canticle *ends with a request to God to perfect the union of the soul by taking it with him to eternal life. Thus, longing to prove that it is ready to take that flight, the soul professes its detachment from all creatures in this humble prayer:*

My soul is now divested, detached, alone, and withdrawn from all created things, both from those above and from those below; and it has entered so deeply into interior recollection with You that none of them can discern the intimate delight I now possess in You; that is, these creatures cannot move my soul to relish their sweetness or become displeased and disturbed by their misery and lowness. Since my soul stays so far from them and abides in such profound delight with You, none of them can get a view of me.

(*Canticle*, 40:2)

84.

Since dialogue is something essential to authentic prayer, the speaker does not always have to be God. In fact, the interlocutor can be any creature questioned about God, as we have already seen in the poems. This also appears in that vigorous and honest commentary in prose to the second song:

Tell my Beloved . . . since I suffer and He alone is my joy, to give me joy; and, since I die and He alone is my life, to give me life.

(*Canticle*, 2:8)

85.

On the other hand, in the commentary to stanza 39, the author beautifully and passionately summons every soul to give themselves entirely to God so that they may be able to say about themselves:

O souls, created for these grandeurs and called to them! What are you doing? How are you spending your time? Your aims are base and your possessions miseries! O wretched blindness of your eyes! You are blind to so brilliant a light and deaf to such loud voices, because you fail to discern that insofar as you seek eminence and glory you remain miserable, base, ignorant, and unworthy of so many blessings!

(*Canticle*, 39:7)

PRAYERS OF ADMIRATION AND PRAISE

Within the category of colloquial prayer—of loving dialogue with God—a whole chapter should be dedicated to a series of prayers in the book of *Flame* that have some peculiar characteristics common to the entire poem. These fragments present the Saint's most passionate stanzas and may be defined as "prayers of admiration and praise." They describe the two most intimate feelings that motivate such prayers in our soul: the admiration and praise for all that God is capable of doing for the benefit of our souls as the unmistakable pledge of his incredible love. To such an extent do such irrepressible feelings take possession of our soul that, knowing them to be ineffable, we resort to an expressive word of admiration. In fact, every stanza and every expression from the author's heart starts with the interjection "O" used repeatedly to express his praise and admiration. The saint himself describes his admiration as follows: "To lay stress on the sentiment and esteem with which it speaks in these four stanzas, the soul uses in all of them the exclamations, 'O' and 'how,' which stress affection. Each time they are uttered, they reveal more about the interior than the tongue expresses. 'O' serves to express intense desire and to use persuasion in petitioning. The soul uses the expression for both reasons" (*Flame*, 1:2). The entire poem that follows offers us the prayer and longing of a soul anxious to burn in the love of God, to whom it sings with everlasting passion. The vibration of each stanza in this necessarily brief poem is so ardent that the soul cannot sustain itself any longer without being shattered by the emotional stress of the experience.

86.

O living flame of love
That tenderly wounds my soul
In its deepest center! Since
Now You are not oppressive,
Now Consummate! if it be Your will:
Tear through the veil of this sweet encounter!

87.

O sweet cautery,
O delightful wound!
O gentle hand! O delicate touch
That tastes of eternal life
And pays every debt!
In killing You changed death to life.

88.

O lamps of fire!
In whose splendors
The deep caverns of feeling,
Once obscure and blind,
Now give forth, so rarely, so exquisitely,
Both warmth and light to their Beloved.

89.

How gently and lovingly
You wake in my heart,
Where in secret You dwell alone;
And by Your sweet breathing,
Filled with good and glory,
How tenderly You swell my heart with love!

90.

Moreover, there is a commentary written in prose which, as the Saint acknowledges in his prologue to Doña Ana de Peñalosa,

*stems from a new spiritual experience, "now that the Lord seems
to have spoken and irradiated his warmth." Thus, the following
two prayers stem from this first stanza, addressed to both the fire
and the wound, as the personification of the Holy Spirit:*

"O living flame of love that tenderly wounds my soul." This is like
saying: O enkindled love, with your loving movements you are
pleasantly glorifying me according to the greater capacity and
strength of my soul, bestowing divine knowledge according to all
the ability and capacity of my intellect, and communicating love
according to the greater power of my will, and rejoicing the substance of my soul with the torrent of your delight by your divine
contact and substantial union, in harmony with the greater purity
of my substance and the capacity and breadth of my memory!

(Flame, 1:17)

91.

O flame of the Holy Spirit that so intimately and tenderly pierces
the substance of my soul and cauterizes it with Your glorious ardor!
Previously, my requests did not reach Your ears, when, in the
anxieties and weariness of love in which my sense and my spirit
suffered because of considerable weakness, impurity, and lack of
strong love, I was praying that You loose me and bring me to
Yourself, because my soul longed for You, and impatient love did
not allow me to be so conformed to the conditions of this life in
which you desired me still to live. The previous impulses of love
were not enough, because they did not have sufficient quality for
the attainment of my desire; now I am so fortified in love that not
only do my sense and spirit no longer faint in You, but my heart and
my flesh, reinforced in You, rejoice in the living God (Ps 83:3), with
great conformity between the sensory and spiritual parts. What you
desire me to ask for, I ask for; and what you do not desire, I do not
desire, nor can I, nor does it even enter my mind to desire it. My
petitions are now more valuable and estimable in Your sight, since
they come from You, and You move me to make them, and I make
them in the delight and joy of the Holy Spirit, my judgment now
issuing from Your countenance (Ps 16:2), that is, when You esteem
and hear my prayer. Tear then the thin veil of this life and do not let

old age cut it naturally, that from now on I may love You with plenitude and fullness my soul desires forever and ever.

(Flame, 1:36)

92.

Curiously, the spiritual experience from which the commentary originates grows in a crescendo until it reaches its highest intensity in the second stanza, at which point the writer expresses his deepest feelings and imploration. Sometimes he speaks to his own soul, as in the following passage:

Oh, the great glory of you who have merited this supreme fire! It is certain that, though it does not destroy you (for it has the infinite force to consume and annihilate you), it does consume you immensely in glory. Do not wonder that God brings some souls to this high peak. The sun is distinguished by some of its marvelous effects.

(Flame, 2:5)

93.

At times the author addresses the wound caused by the Flame of the Spirit, as in the song of praise that follows:

O happy wound, wrought by one who knows only how to heal! O fortunate and choicest wound; you were made only for delight, and the quality of your affliction is delight and gratification for the wounded soul! You are great, O delightful wound, because He who caused you is great! And your delight is great, because the fire of love is infinite and makes you delightful according to your capacity and greatness. O, then, delightful wound, so much more sublimely delightful the more the cautery touched the intimate center of the substance of the soul, burning all that was burnable in order to give delight to all that could be delighted!

(Flame, 2:8)

94.

Then he talks to the Father, admiring the infinite generosity and tenderness he bestows upon every soul. It is a magnificent prayer, filled with biblical innuendos and references:

O hand, You are as gentle to my soul, which you touch by resting gently, as You would be powerful enough to submerge the entire world if You rested somewhat heavily, for by Your look alone the earth trembles (Ps 103:32), the nations melt and faint, and the mountains crumble! (Hb 3:6). Oh, then again, great hand, by touching Job somewhat roughly, You were as hard and rigorous with him (Jb 19:21) as You are friendly and gentle with me; how much more lovingly, graciously, and gently do You permanently touch my soul! You cause death, and You give life, and no one flees from Your hand. For You, O divine life, never wound unless to heal. When You chastise, Your touch is gentle, but it is enough to destroy the world. When You give delight, You rest very firmly, and thus the delight of Your sweetness is immeasurable. You have wounded me in order to cure me, O divine hand, and You have put to death in me what made me lifeless, deprived me of God's life in which I now see myself live. You granted this with the liberality of Your generous grace, which You used in contacting me with the touch of the splendor of Your glory and the figure of Your substance (Heb 1:3), which is Your only begotten Son, through Whom, being Your substance, You touch mightily from one end to the other (Wis 8:1).

(Flame, 2:16)

95.

Still, the most vibrant and inflamed prayers are found in his dialogue with Christ, where he experiences the delicate touch of the Father's hand helping his creatures. The sequence of these Christological prayers opens with this intense invocation:

O You, then, delicate touch, the Word, the Son of God, through the delicacy of Your divine being, You subtly penetrate the substance of my soul and, lightly touching it all, absorb it entirely in Yourself in divine modes of delights and sweetnesses unheard of in the land of Canaan and never before seen in Theman! (Bar 3:22). O, then, very delicate, exceedingly delicate, touch of the Word, so much the more delicate for me insofar as, after overthrowing the mountains and smashing the rocks to pieces on Mount Horeb with the shadow of might and power that went before You, You gave the prophet the sweetest and strongest experience of Yourself in

the gentle breeze! (3 Kgs 19:11-12). O gentle breeze, since You are
a delicate and mild breeze, tell us: How do you, the Word, the Son
of God, touch mildly and gently, since You are so awesome and
mighty?

(Flame, 2:17)

96.

*In the following paragraph the author intermingles both his
prayer to Christ with that to the Father, asking the latter to reveal
his love and presence in the Son. Paradoxically, he also begs him
not to do so, lest he might undervalue his generosity:*

Oh, happy is the soul that You, being terrible and strong, gently
and lightly touch! Proclaim this to the world! but You are unwilling
to proclaim this to the world because it does not know of a mild
breeze and will not experience You, for it can neither receive nor
see You (Jn 14:17). But they, O my God and my life, will see and
experience Your mild touch, who withdraw from the world and
become mild, bringing the mild into harmony with the mild, thus
enabling themselves to experience and enjoy You. You touch them
the more gently the more You dwell permanently hidden within
them, for the substance of their soul is now refined, cleansed, and
purified, withdrawn from every creature and every touch and trace
of creature. As a result, *You hide them in the secret of Your face,*
which is the Word, *from the disturbance of men* (Ps 30:21).

(Flame, 2:17)

97.

*Once more he addresses Christ, whose love surpasses any other
possible love. We can all apply this prayer to ourselves, as long as
we are convinced of this truth and ask the Lord to grant us the
grace of his love.*

O, then again, repeatedly delicate touch, so much the stronger
and mightier the more You are delicate, since You detach and
withdraw the soul from all the other touches of created things by
the might of Your delicacy, and reserve it for and unite it to Yourself

alone, so mild an effect do You leave in the soul that every other touch of all things both high and low seems coarse and spurious. It displeases the soul to look at these things, and to deal with them is a heavy pain and torment to it.

(*Flame*, 2:18)

98.

It seems, however, that the Saint is not satisfied with merely giving vent to his feelings and therefore turns to prayer, using repeatedly the aforementioned interjection of wonder:

O then, delicate touch, the more abundantly You pervade my soul, the more substantial You are and the purer is my soul! It should also be known that the more subtle and delicate the touch, and the more delight and gratification it communicates there where it touches, the less volume and bulk it has. This divine touch has no bulk or volume, because the Word who grants it is alien to every mode and manner, and free from all the volume of form, figure, and accident which usually encircles and imposes boundaries or limits to the substance. Finally, then, O Word, indescribably delicate touch, produced in the soul only by Your most simple being, which, since it is infinite, is infinitely delicate and hence touches so subtly, lovingly, eminently, and delicately! That tastes of eternal life.

(*Flame*, 2:19, 20, 21)

99.

At the end of the commentary to this stanza the author invokes the Holy Spirit as the medicine and the delicate touch of Christ:

Oh, fine cure that burns infinitely more than any fire, the more you burn the gentler you are to me! Oh pleasant wound, you are my health, beyond any other health in the world! Oh soft hand that is softer the more firmly it presses me. Oh delicate touch whose gentleness far exceeds the delicacy and beauty of all creatures. You are sweeter and more delicious than honey and the honey-comb since your taste is that of eternal life. And the more intimately you touch me the more I can taste it. It is infinitely more precious than gold and precious stones since with it you pay for our debts, which nothing else in the world can cancel, since you admirably transform death into life.

(Flame, 2:31)

100.

The Saint demands, complains, begs and urges all souls to allow themselves to be loved and burned by God's love:

O souls who in spiritual matters desire to walk in security and consolation! If you but knew how much it behooves you to suffer in order to reach this security and consolation, and how, without suffering, you cannot attain to your desire, but rather turn back, in nowise would you look for comfort either from God or from creatures. You would instead carry the cross and, placed upon it, desire to drink the pure gall and vinegar. You would consider it good fortune that, upon dying to this world and to yourselves, you would live to God in the delights of the spirit, and that patiently and faithfully suffering exterior trials, which are small, you would merit that God fix His eyes on you and purge you more profoundly through deeper spiritual trials in order to give you more interior blessings.

(Flame, 2:28)

101.

After these vibrant expressions, the Saint relaxes his commentary and the prayers become scarce. There are only three in the third stanza, and one in the fourth. The first two are a dialogue with God, whose attributes are exalted by the author:

O marvelous thing, that the soul at this time is flooded with divine waters, abounding in them like a plentiful fount overflowing on all sides!

(Flame, 3:8)

102.

O wonderful excellence of God! Since these lamps of the divine attributes are a simple being and are enjoyed only in Him, they are seen and enjoyed distinctly, each one as enkindled as the other, and each substantially the other. O abyss of delights! You are so much the more abundant the more Your riches are concentrated in the infinite unity and simplicity of Your unique being, where one attribute is so known and enjoyed as not to hinder the perfect knowledge and enjoyment of the other; rather, each grace and virtue within You is a light for each of Your other grandeurs. By Your purity, O divine Wisdom, many things are beheld in You through one. For You are the deposit of the Father's treasures.

(Flame, 3:17)

103.

In the third prayer the author maintains a dialogue with his readers, inviting them to abandon their carnal ways and benefit from God's work in them:

O, then, souls, when God is according you such sovereign favors as to lead you by the state of solitude and recollection, withdrawing you from the labors of the senses, do not revert to the senses. Abandon your activity, for if this helped you, when you were beginners, to deny the world and yourselves, now that God favors you by being Himself the agent, it is a serious obstacle. God will feed you with heavenly refreshment since you do not apply your faculties to anything, nor encumber them, but detach them from everything, which is all you yourself have to do (besides the simple loving attentiveness in the way I mentioned above, that is, when you feel no aversion toward it). You should not use any force, except to detach the soul and liberate it, so as not to alter its peace and tranquillity.

(Flame, 3:65)

104.

In the last prayer, which is a warning rather than an entreaty, the Saint expresses his admiration for those that have arrived at the stage of tranquility in God, urging them to remain in that quietude:

Oh, how happy is this soul which ever experiences God resting and reposing within it! Oh, how fitting it is for it to withdraw from things, flee from business matters, and live in immense tranquility, so that it may not even with the slightest mote or noise disturb or trouble its heart where the Beloved dwells.

(Flame, 4:15)

105.

These prayers of admiration and praise do not belong exclusively to the book of the Flame, *even though it is there that they abound the most and bear a special meaning. However, it is almost an exception to find them in other works. In the commentary to stanza 12 of the* Spiritual Canticle, *we come across the following inflamed dialogues:*

O faith of Christ, my Spouse, would that you might show me clearly now the truths of my Beloved, which you have infused in my soul and which are covered with obscurity and darkness (for faith, as the theologians say, is an obscure habit), in such a way that, what you communicate to me in inexplicit and obscure knowledge, you would show suddenly, clearly, and perfectly, changing it into a manifestation of glory!

(Canticle, 12:2)

106.

Oh, if only on your silvered-over face (the articles we mentioned) by which you cover the gold of the divine rays (the eyes I have desired), and she adds: You would suddenly form the eyes I have desired.

(Canticle, 12:4)

107.

Oh, if only the truths hidden in your articles, which you teach me in an inexplicit and dark manner, you would give me now completely, clearly, and explicitly, freed of their covering, as my desire begs!

(Canticle, 12:5)

108.

There is another precious pearl which is not accompanied by the usual interjection but appears unexpectedly in the commentary to stanza 36, in which the soul indulges itself in praising and desiring the beauty of God:

Let us so act that by means of this loving activity we may attain to the vision of ourselves in Your beauty in eternal life. That is: That I be so transformed in Your beauty that we may be alike in beauty, and both behold ourselves in Your beauty, possessing now Your very beauty; this, in such a way that each looking at the other may see in the other his own beauty, since both are Your beauty alone, I being absorbed in Your beauty; hence, I shall see You in Your beauty, and You shall see me in Your beauty, and I shall see myself in You in Your beauty, and You will see Yourself in me in Your beauty; that I may resemble You in Your beauty, and You resemble me in Your beauty, and my beauty be Your beauty and Your beauty my beauty: wherefore I shall be You in Your beauty, and You will be me in Your beauty, because Your very beauty will be my beauty; and therefore we shall behold each other in Your beauty.

(Canticle, 36:5)

109.

Finally, in chapter 16 of the second book of the Night, *while explaining that the soul is secure even when walking in the dark, the author expresses this beautiful soliloquy-lamentation about the insecurities and dangers every creature must endure. Since this condition is suffered by every believer, it is a prayer common to us all:*

Oh, what a miserable lot this life is! We live in the midst of so much danger and find it so hard to arrive at truth. The clearest and truest things are the darkest and most dubious to us and consequent-

ly we flee from what most suits us. We embrace what fills our eyes
with the most light and satisfaction and run after what is the very
worst thing for us, and we fall at every step. In how much danger
and fear does man live, since the very light of his natural eyes which
ought to be his guide is the first to deceive him in his journey to
God and since he must keep his eyes shut and tread the path in
darkness if he wants to be sure of where he is going and be
safeguarded against the enemies of his house, his senses and faculties.

(*2 Night*, 16:12)

110.

In the commentary to stanza 36 of the Canticle *the Saint gives
vent to similar feelings in relation to the need to suffer. This prayer
can be used to ask the Lord to help us search his wisdom and the
richness of his cross:*

Oh! If we could but now fully understand how a soul cannot
reach the thicket and wisdom of the riches of God, which are of
many kinds, without entering the thicket of many kinds of suffering,
finding in this her delight and consolation; and how a soul with an
authentic desire for divine wisdom, wants suffering first in order to
enter this wisdom by the thicket of the cross!

(*Canticle*, 36:13)

GOD'S RESPONSE

We said before that authentic prayer is always a loving dialogue between the soul and God. It is in this meeting that our soul has the best and only chance of coming out of itself and communicating its feelings, as well as of receiving the help it needs to fulfill its life with serenity. We have also seen how the soul expresses its feelings to the Lord, confident in his warm and communicative presence. In fact, God always responds to the prayer of those who confide in him. Still, he does not usually talk to us in our own language but through the word revealed in his scriptures, which we can only perceive when there is silence in our hearts.

However, the mystics and Saint John himself tell us that sometimes God does use our language to talk to us. Saint John believes this language is made up of formal and substantial words through which God works in our souls to reach his goal. Occasionally, however, God speaks to us through "successive" words which stem from our understanding when reflecting upon a given truth, which should not be expressly attributed to him.

Since God does not usually communicate in this fashion, the best we can do is try to understand through our silence and faith what he wishes to tell us through everyday events and his revealed word, mainly the word of our brothers and sisters, so commonly used by God to reveal himself.

However, we usually find it difficult to pay attention to that kind of message from God. We seldom give him the chance to speak as we fail to create the necessary silence since we are too anxious to express our own feelings.

Saint John, however, was a man capable of keeping intense silence and attention. In fact, he provided us with a series of brief prayers representing God's response to his listeners, which we do not always perceive due to our inability to listen with pure faith.

Some of them are found in stanza 13 of the *Spiritual Canticle*, and are loving dialogues between the soul and its Lord.

111.

Return, dove, for the communication you receive from Me is not yet of the state of glory to which you now aspire. Return to Me, for I am He Whom you, wounded with love, seek. For I too, like the stag, wounded by your love begin to reveal Myself to you in your high contemplation, and I am refreshed and renewed in the love which arises from your contemplation.

(Canticle, 13:2)

112.

Return from this lofty flight in which you aim after true possession of Me; the time has not yet come for such a high knowledge, adapt yourself to this lower knowledge which I am communicating to you in this rapture of yours.

(Canticle, 13:8)

113.

Return to Me, My bride, because if you go like the stag wounded with love for Me, I too, like the stag, will come to you wounded by your wound.

(Canticle, 13:9)

114.

Similar fragments can be found in the Ascent of Mount Carmel, *which is the least effusive of John's books. In chapter 22 the author presents two staunch and beautiful responses from God the Father to those who divert themselves in searching and expecting a revelation other than the word spoken by Christ to their hearts. Thus, the Father says to us:*

If I have already told you all things in My Word, My Son, and if I have no other word, what answer or revelation can I now make that would surpass this? Fasten your eyes on Him alone, because in Him I have spoken and revealed all, and in Him you shall discover even more than you ask for and desire. You are making an appeal for locutions and revelations that are incomplete, but if you turn your

eyes to Him you will find them complete. For he is My entire
locution and response, vision and revelation, which I have already
spoken, answered, manifested, and revealed to you, by giving Him
to you as a brother, companion, master, ransom, and reward. Since
that day when I descended upon Him with My Spirit on Mount
Tabor proclaiming: *Hic est filius meus dilectus in quo mihi bene
complacui, ipsum audite* (This is my Beloved Son in Whom I am
well pleased, hear Him) (Mt 17:5), I have relinquished these
methods of answering and teaching, and presented them to Him.
Hear Him because I have no more faith to reveal nor truths to
manifest. If I spoke before, it was to promise Christ; if they questioned Me, their inquiries were related to their petitions and longings for Christ in Whom they were to obtain every good (as is
evidenced in all the doctrine of the Evangelists and Apostles). But
now anyone asking Me in that way and desiring that I speak and
reveal something to him would somehow be requesting Christ
again, and more faith, yet he would be failing in faith, because Christ
has already been given. Accordingly, he would offend My Beloved
Son deeply, because he would not merely be lacking faith in Him,
but obliging Him to become incarnate and undergo His life and
death again. You shall not find anything to ask or desire through
revelations and visions; behold Him well, for in Him you will
uncover all these revelations already made, and many more.

(2 Ascent, 22:5)

115.

If you desire Me to answer with a word of comfort, behold My
Son, subject to Me and to others out of love for Me, and you will see
how much he answers. If you desire Me to declare some secret
truths or events to you, fix your eyes on Him, and you will discern
hidden in Him the most secret mysteries, and wisdom, and the
wonders of God, as My Apostle proclaims: *In quo sunt omnes
thesauri sapientiae et scientiae Dei absconditi* (In the son of God
are hidden all the treasures of the wisdom and knowledge of God)
(Col 2:3). These treasures of wisdom and knowledge will be far
more sublime, delightful, and advantageous than what you want to
know. The Apostle, therefore, gloried, affirming that he had acted
as though he knew no other than Jesus Christ and Him crucified (1

Cor 2:2). And if you should seek other divine or corporal visions and revelations, behold Him, become human, and you will encounter more than you imagine, because the Apostle also says: *In ipso habitat omnis plenitudo Divinitatis corporaliter* (In Christ all the fullness of the divinity dwells bodily) (Col 2:9).

(2 Ascent, 22:6)

After this journey through Saint John's writings, which are certainly not exhaustive, one thing appears to be clear: the Saint has unintentionally given us a living example of how our prayer, our colloquial communication with God should be. Consequently, we have been able to penetrate his dialogue with God in more detail and examine the tone of his personal prayer to which, as his contemporaries tell us, he dedicated so many hours of his life amidst the most diverse circumstances.

Thus, we shall be better able now to understand the scope of his doctrine on prayer.

2.

Doctrine on Prayer

INTRODUCTION

After having listened to the living echo of Saint John's dialogue with the Lord, and given the fact of his celebrity as a writer, anyone would believe he was an expert in prayer in the strictest sense of the word. That is, a theorist, a specialist who wrote deep and solid pages on the mystery of Christian prayer.

However, in order to avoid being surprised or disappointed we should be warned immediately that this is not the case. In fact, even if prayer occupied the center of his life, it was not at the center of his doctrinal teaching. None of his spiritual treatises, for which he has justly received the title of Doctor of the Church, were aimed at analyzing prayer in itself, as well as its process, demands, stages, pedagogy, etc. Nor is it accurate to say that he studied the question of prayer in depth, even though he acknowledges its capital importance as an irreplaceable means to relate to God in the process of our spiritual pilgrimage through life based on faith. Futhermore, Saint John considered prayer as an extremely important means to reach union with God, which is the goal of our spiritual journey, and therefore chose prayer as the main theme of his writings.

An approach to Saint John's doctrine

Upon starting to write, Saint John points out that his purpose is not to repeat what others have already said or write about those topics on which there is already "plentiful doctrine" and "written things" (*1 Night*, 8:2) as it is clearly in the case of prayer. He intends rather to cast some light on those subjects about which "little has been said," such as the need our soul has of the "Night," that is the active and passive purification of both our senses and our spirit. This is a topic about which the Saint wrote extensively and is precisely the subject of two of his treatises: the *Ascent of Mount Carmel* and the *Dark Night of the Soul*. On the other hand, his written teachings were addressed to immediate and specific people, such as his brothers and sisters in the Discalced order, monks and nuns or other concrete individuals, as in the *Canticle* and the *Flame*. It is also evident that his listeners were familiar with the theme of prayer. For them, prayer was something known and practiced about which they did not require precise instructions. This enabled the Saint to concentrate on the more novel and suggestive theme of the *Night*.

This means, in practice, two factual things. First, that the Saint wrote for people who already lived the experience of prayer and did not require any introduction to the subject, and secondly, that his readers were people who already knew the mechanisms and processes of prayer. Thus, they did not need a detailed explanation of a topic they were well acquainted with from their own experience.

Prayer as the means to union

Now, the fact that the Saint did not tackle the question of prayer directly and in depth does not mean that he did not refer frequently to it in his writings, among other topics. Furthermore, we can say without exaggeration that in many of his writings the topic of prayer lies as a backdrop since even though he did not refer often to prayer explicitly he frequently referred to it indirectly. And truly, it could not have been otherwise since the ultimate objective of his doctrine is to achieve union with God. His teaching consists in warning and reminding us that God has given us his grace and has called us to him. And our union with God can be reached precisely through the privileged gift of prayer, which is the usual means we may resort to relate to God throughout our pilgrimage on earth. This union with God often stems from the loving encounter of contemplation, the culmination of Christian prayer.

Therefore, from this perspective it is not surprising that rather than referring to prayer as a discursive exercise of meditation, as it is usually described in spiritual treatises, Saint John should speak about the peak of prayer, that is contemplation. In fact, his references to contemplation are quite explicit and plentiful in his writings as a guidance and guarantee to those who search for and live by it. He insisted on this subject since, as we said before, he did not want to repeat what was common and addressed those who were not content with their usual prayer but aimed at reaching the state of contemplation, such as the Discalced nuns and monks and those who were in need of guidance due to the scarcity of doctrine available on this topic.

The subject of contemplation

After all, we could conclude that Saint John's doctrine on prayer is not so meager as it may seem to us since it abounds in references to contemplation, which is, in fact, a form of prayer. Contemplation implies a deeper relationship with God, which propitiates the union, the ultimate goal of Saint John's doctrine. However, since contemplation is a specific manner of prayer granted by God to whom he pleases and which cannot be reached by our sole individual efforts, we do not wish to linger upon this subject but rather see how prayer was at the center of the Saint's life and gather those aspects of his doctrine that are useful to everyone, irrespective of what God wishes to accomplish through his grace in each of us. However, in some cases his references to contemplation are so closely linked to that of prayer that it is impossible to talk about one without referring to the other, of which the former is its climax. Likewise, it is not easy to draw a bordering line between both realities in the vital experience of the soul that has reached that stage.

Prayer, the search for God

Bearing all this in mind as a premise to examining Saint John's philosophy on prayer, we realize that he was not actually concerned about offering an exact definition of prayer, though we do know what prayer meant to him from his many references to the topic. Saint John draws a clear distinction between vocal prayer, the recitation of compound prayers that we make our own, and meditative prayer which is "a discursive act built upon forms, figures, and images, imagined and fashioned by these senses," the imagination and the phantasy (*2 Ascent*, 12:3).

To better understand the above, he offers a concrete example: "The imagining of Christ crucified, or at the column, or in some other scene; or of God seated upon a throne with resplendent majesty; or the imagining and considering of glory as a beautiful light, etc.; or the picturing of any other human or divine object imaginable" (*ibid.*).

Now, this imaginative speech about God is by no means a purely intellectual exercise, as when we reflect upon certain human realities or try to deepen in the speculative knowledge of a given truth, judgment or reasoning. The aim of Christian meditation has always been quite different from that of pure reflection. In fact, Christian meditation attempts to establish a connection and an encounter with God himself, even if this can only be done through our faith. That is what the Saint is in fact telling us, with no beating about the bush. He points out that meditation is "discursive meditation, in which an individual begins his quest for God" (*2 Ascent*, 17:7) which means, clearly and simply, that prayer is an occasion and a means to meet God and, therefore, our desire to pray stems from our longing for that encounter. Moreover, the only substantial reason that makes us resort to prayer is our desire to converse with, relate to, and meet God, which is something quite different from making theological statements about his divine nature or attributes.

Prayer, a loving exercise

In his approach to a possible definition of prayer and pointing to an important shade in the tone of the imaginative discourse we follow in our meditation, the Saint had previously said "that the purpose of discursive meditation on divine subjects is the acquisition of some knowledge and love of God (*2 Ascent*, 14:2).

Thus, it becomes clear once more that "discourse" is not an

intellectual but an emotional exercise. Therefore, the search and exercise in meditation is nothing but the search and exercise in the love of God. In fact, the Saint believes that when this is done more often and grows into a habit, the love of God becomes more inherent and permanent. This is achieved more fully when God takes our soul to the state of contemplation which, according to Saint John, is nothing but "loving, peaceful, and tranquil knowledge, drinking wisdom and love and delight (*ibid.*).

Prayer, silence and listening

According to the Saint, however, before reaching the enjoyment of this love and the tranquillity that stems from contemplation, there is a threshold where our soul must abandon meditation, at which point we describe the latter as "a general message or loving summons by God" (*ibid.*).

Thus, it is clear that prayer, as John understood it and practiced it, is nothing but a loving encounter between the creature and God. It is an exercise in the loving summons of mutual love, of the kind of love we receive from God and feel driven to respond to.

Saint John says that in order to make that "summons" more complete, and therefore more love-inciting, we are required to renounce and detach ourselves from every other thought and experience. He insists in the fact that if we wish to attain the gift of contemplation we should rid ourselves of every impediment. In his *Living Flame of Love,* he describes those engaged in meditative prayer as "individuals who are entranced in deep silence, listening to God speak to their soul" (*Flame*, 3:34).

As in many other treatise writers, he sees prayer as the dialogue the creature tries to maintain through faith with God in order to understand his divine plan, a dialogue that inflames their mutual communication, as well as their friendship, love and communion.

Prayer, the means to reach union with God

Having discovered prayer as that intimate, personal, loving and uniting encounter, it is understandable why the Saint has excluded from his teaching all that is not relevant to this subject. We can see, in fact, why he has not referred to praying methods or dynamics or the most significant stretches of our spiritual experience, which would have helped us to become acquainted with the different stages of our journey, enabling us to know where we stand at any given time. His concern is that we may fail to reach union with God for not purifying our spirit; divert our attention towards accessory things with which to nourish our hearts while depriving ourselves from reaching and establishing communion with God.

Hence, the Saint pauses to talk to us about the conditions for true prayer and how to attain its purpose, so that we do not remain unsatisfied in a never-ending search of God. Moreover, he discourages us from maintaining a dialogue with God that while affectionate may be superficial whenever we engage in simultaneous conversations and relationships with other creatures that hinder our soul's union with God. This requires:

— pureness of heart (3 Ascent, 40:2), which means that we respond to our search with a heart cleansed from its sins and with no other desire than God.

— solitude (3 Ascent, 36:3), so that we may not get entangled in the bustle of voices or companies other than God.

— inner recollection (ibid.), so that we may rejoice in being alone with him, without being distracted by external things.

— freedom of spirit (3 Flame, 34) or self-detachment, so that we may not be attached to anything that could prevent our soul from reaching contemplation.

Prayer as an encounter and experience of faith

However, the most important requirement for reaching full union with God through prayer, is the following:

— a living faith with nothing else to lean on (3 Ascent, 36) since faith is the "only and suitable means to attain union" (2 Ascent, 28:1).

All this is dealt with in more detail by the Saint, as we shall later see when making a selection of his philosophy and doctrine on prayer, consistent with his principle of teaching those topics about which little has been said rather than about those things that have been dealt with plentifully, a fact due perhaps to a lack of discernment in many authors in distinguishing what is essential from what is accessory in prayer. This the Saint does especially in the last chapter of the third book of the *Ascent of Mount Carmel,* which, as its previous chapters, describes the process of purification of our will, a theme included in the *Night.*

In those same chapters the Saint expands on the subject of vocal prayer, the kind of prayer that most Christians practice. However, due to the Saint's tendency to concentrate on what is most profound and substantial, he tries to warn his followers not to seek only the pleasures of prayer or be distracted by its external appearance, however desirable and helpful it may appear to us. He advises us to search what is essential and pray exactly as Christ taught us. He then makes a subtle analysis, an actual X-ray of the environmental setting in which he moves and prays and the danger of going astray for paying more attention to external things rather than to the intimate disposition of his soul. He believes that, above all, our faith should have no external support, the most important condition to engage in actual prayer, both vocal and meditative.

We shall presently examine the actual fragments in which the Saint warns and censures those who get entangled in accessory things such as oratories and ceremonies.

Saint John's condensed teaching on vocal and mental prayer can be grouped in the following subjects. First, a series of brief considerations on the value of prayer. Secondly, the aforementioned requirements for true prayer. Thirdly, that special ordeal we undergo in prayer, that is the feeling of dryness, which is the great chance given to our soul to purify itself, the opportunity given to beginners to experience the night. Finally, the writer offers us a series of directions on how to do without meditation once our soul has reached the threshold of contemplation.

Master of contemplation

Once establishing what is most important in Saint John's doctrine on prayer we should try, however, not to dwarf the richness of his teaching since these pages only gather his references to meditation and prayer at large. On the other hand, the subject of contemplation on which he abounds, surpasses the scope of this book. Saint John is certainly a master of prayer due to his testimony, experience and doctrine on the subject. For the sake of precision, however, we must say that in reality the Saint was a contemplative man of incomparable stature, as well as a master of contemplation. He was a teacher who spoke to contemplatives and urged his listeners to become contemplatives as well. He was convinced that even though the state of contemplation is purely grace, or "a message infused by God, which enlightens and enraptures our soul" (*2 Night,* 18:5) the Lord does not refuse it to those who search it in earnest through meditative prayer, provided the latter is founded on substantial and not just accidental things, and provided they are not prevented by the ignorance of certain spiritual masters from making progress and reaching the summit of prayer, which is contemplation.

Contemplation, a vital attitude

According to the Saint, rather than a genre of prayer meditation is a vital and theological attitude of permanent reference to God. It is a way of living and acting at every moment and circumstance of our lives. An attitude that both stems from and leads to that contemplative prayer the soul should exercise whenever possible to allow itself to become inflamed by the "loving message from God," establishing a communication with him that will eventually lead to that longed-for union. This vital contemplative attitude is so closely intertwined with our own contemplative prayer that both realities overlap. Such is the case regarding our attitude of interior emotional recollection, which above all entails our having found the center and focal point of life in our own heart, in our personal encounter and communion with God and his love. Hence, in him all the implied energies and desires to overcome our scattered affections are integrated. As the Saint masterly describes it, "in God the strength of our will is reunited" (*3 Ascent,* 28:6).

And this is another characteristic that identifies a genuine contemplative. Contemplatives are men or women who live as everyone else, people who are engaged in conflicting occupations and wrapped in daily worries. Still, their lives are centered in God and they do not scatter their energies or affections over the objects and people surrounding them, but are committed to the permanent growth of their love and communion with God.

In reality, since contemplation is the peak and logical goal of an earnest experience of prayer, a "loving habit" as Saint John would say, stemming from meditation, these two elements should not be in contradiction with each other nor should we be contented with staying at the early steps of meditation without ever reaching the summit.

Were we to make a more exhaustive analysis of what contemplative prayer means according to Saint John of the Cross, what has been said so far would not suffice. However, since our purpose here is less ambitious and consists in gathering the most substantial elements of his doctrine on prayer, what we have said so far will suffice to better understand the tone, meaning and scope of his philosophy.

THE VALUE OF PRAYER

In this first section of Saint John's writings there is a series of short maxims pondering the value of prayer. Most of them are taken from his individual admonishments to nuns or monks for their personal guidance. While each admonishment has a concrete, personal and intimate context, we ignore the exact circumstances that gave origin to them and their addressees. We do know, however, that these timely and knowledgeable pieces of advice are applicable to other situations as well.

Yet, the doctrine enclosed in the Saint's admonishments is described later in his books, which constitute a synthesis of his teaching on different matters, including prayer.

The following are a few examples of these admonishments.

1.

Whoever flees prayer flees all that is good.

(Counsels, 11)

2.

Preserve a loving attentiveness to God with no desire to feel or understand any particular thing concerning Him.

(Maxims, 9)

3.

It is a serious evil to have more regard for God's blessings than for God Himself: prayer and detachment.

(Maxims, 59)

4.

God values in you an inclination to aridity and suffering for love of Him more than all possible consolation, spiritual visions, and meditations.

(Sayings, 14)

5.

Seek in reading and you will find in meditation; knock in prayer and it will be opened to you in contemplation.

(Maxims, 79)

6.

The fly that clings to honey hinders its flight, and the soul that allows itself attachment to spiritual sweetness hinders its own liberty and contemplation.

(Sayings, 24)

7.

What you most seek and desire you will not find by this way of yours, nor through high contemplation, but in much humility and submission of heart.

(Sayings, 37)

8.

Twelve stars for reaching the highest perfection: love of God, love of neighbor, obedience, chastity, poverty, attendance at choir, penance, humility, mortification, prayer, silence, peace.

(Maxims, 77)

9.

Do not omit mental prayer for any occupation, for it is the sustenance of your soul.

(Degrees, 5)

10.

Never give up prayer, and should you find dryness and difficulty, persevere in it for this very reason. God often desires to see what love your soul has, and love is not tried by ease and satisfaction.

(Degrees, 9)

11.

While only seldom, we can detect similar admonishments in the Saint's major works, which seem to be addressed to someone in particular but actually belong to a more extensive and detailed context. Such is the case of this and the following:

In all our necessities, trials, and difficulties, no better or safer aid exists for us than prayer and hope that God will provide for us by the means He desires.

(3 Ascent, 21:5)

12.

The soul should persevere in prayer and should hope in the midst of nakedness and emptiness, for its blessings will not be long in coming.

(3 Ascent, 3:6)

13.

A man who must overcome the devil's strength will be unable to do so without prayer, nor will he be able to understand his deceits without mortification and humility.

(Canticle, 3:9)

14.

As an exception to the rule, the concepts conveyed by the admonishments are sometimes more elaborate and surpass the definition of spiritual maxims since they deal with wider doctrinal topics. However, most of the elaborate thoughts explained at length by the author in his main works concern prayer and the attitudes that should accompany prayer. This and the following are examples of such admonishments:

If you desire to discover peace and consolation for your soul and serve God truly, do not be content in this that you have left behind (because in that which now concerns you, you may be as impeded as you were before, or even more), but also leave all these other things and attend to one thing alone, which brings all these with it, namely, holy solitude, together with prayer and spiritual and divine reading, and persevere there in forgetfulness of all things. For if these things are not incumbent upon you, you will be more pleasing to God in knowing how to guard and perfect yourself than by gaining all other things together, for what does it profit a man if he gains the whole world and suffers the loss of his soul? (Mt 16:26).

(Sayings, 76)

15.

There are three signs of inner recollection: first, a lack of satisfaction in passing things; second, a liking for solitude and silence and an attentiveness to all that is more perfect; third, the considerations, meditations, and acts which formerly helped the soul now hinder it, and it brings to prayer no other support than faith, hope, and love.

(*Maxims*, 40)

The anagogical acts

16.

Look at that infinite knowledge and that hidden secret. What peace, what love, what silence is in that divine bosom! How lofty the science God teaches there, which is what we call the anagogical acts that so enkindle the heart.

(*Maxims*, 60)

17.

The Saint describes the anagogical acts as efficacious means to inflame the love of God. In this regard, Father Eliseo de los Mártires, one of Saint John's disciples, recalls the Saint's own words:

And their manner of resisting has to be that which entails the most fervent anagogical practices they can do; which they should then repeat a number of times. If it does not suffice, because the temptations are overpowering and they are weak, they should use all the weapons that they find necessary to resist and win, such as well-done meditations and other such acts. They should then know and believe this to be the preferred and truest manner of resisting, because it includes all of the most important and necessary war strategies.

(*Suggestions*, 5)

18.

However, it may be useful to further specify the nature of these anagogical acts and their meaning according to Saint John, since they advance a peculiar kind of prayer recommended by the

Saint. While the text is lengthy, it is worth transcribing it in its entirety:

There is an easier, more fruitful and perfect way to overcome our vices and temptations and acquire the virtues. Our soul, only by its anagogical and loving actions and movements and leaving aside other strange exercises can resist and destroy the temptations presented to us by our enemy and reach the virtues in their most perfect state.

And Saint John believes the above is possible in the following manner:

Whenever we feel the first hint of an assault on us of a vice such as lust, anger, impatience or the spirit of revenge for a wrong done to us, etc., we should resist it with an act of the opposite virtue, that is, resist that given vice with an act of anagogical love, raising our affection to the union with God. In fact, by doing this, the soul leaves that place and presents itself before God, uniting itself to him. Therefore, the vice or temptation presented by the enemy is frustrated and does not harm its victim. In fact, the soul becomes more present to he whom it loves than to the tempter, allowing the body to escape divinely from temptation. Thus, the enemy no longer finds where to strike or whom to capture, because the soul is no longer there where he can inflict its wound.

And then, oh marvelous thing, the soul, as if forgetful of the temptation and united with its Beloved, does not feel any attraction to the vice with which the devil tempts it. As we said before, the soul can do this because it is no longer there, so the enemy is tempting a dead body, fighting with what is no longer there and can not feel.

A heroic and admirable virtue is thus planted in the soul, which Saint Thomas, the angelical Doctor, calls perfectly purged virtue and soul. The Saint says the soul attains such a virtue when God leads it to that state in which it no longer feels the lure of vices, nor their assaults, nor any other temptation. From here stems an extraordinary perfection due to which the soul is always still, whether it is insulted, praised, glorified or humbled, or whether good or evil is spoken of it. In fact, since the anagogical and loving movements lead the soul to such a high and sublime state, the soul forgets everything that is not its Beloved, that is, Jesus Christ.

Thus, since the soul is united to God and occupied with him, the temptations do not find whom to inflict their wounds on, for they cannot reach the height the soul has attained or that God has led it to: "No evil shall befall you" (Ps 91:10).

Then he continues by saying:

Beginners, whose loving and anagogical acts are not fast or swift enough to reach the union of their souls to the spouse with one leap, are advised, when being tempted and the temptation does not subside immediately, to keep resisting with all the weapons and considerations they may think of, until the temptation is completely overcome.

And here is the text mentioned at the beginning:

In short, the anagogical and loving acts contribute to raise our affections to God. Through them we express our longing for union, and they help us divert our attention from our own worries and temptations.

(Suggestions, 5)

Prayer and apostolic zeal

19.

Similar suggestions can be found in relation to prayer and the apostolic zeal prayer produces:

It is an evident truth that compassion for our neighbors grows in as much as our soul unites itself out of love to God. The more we love, the more we desire that God be loved and honored by everyone. And the more we desire this, the more we work for it, be it by prayer or by any other necessary acts. Then, being in God, the zeal and power of our charity becomes always stronger, to the point that that which we gain for ourselves seems too little; it just seems insufficient to go to heaven alone. So, with celestial affection and diligent care we will be able to bring many others along with us. This all stems from our great love for God, and is the fruitful effect of perfect prayer and contemplation.

(Suggestions, 6)

20.

Saint John offers further guidance on the value of prayer and the best way to practice it in his brief treatise consisting of four admonishments to a Carmelite monk. Within the context of the fourth admonishment, which offers advice on solitude and the detachment of our affections from everything that is not God, he explains:

I do not mean here that you fail to fulfill the duties of your state with all necessary and possible care, and any others that obedience commands, but that you execute your tasks in such a way that no fault is committed, for neither God nor obedience wants you to commit a fault.

You should consequently strive to be incessant in prayer, and in the midst of your corporal practices do not abandon it. Whether you eat, or drink, or speak, or converse with lay people, or do anything else, you should always do so with the desire for God and with your heart fixed on Him. This is very necessary for inner solitude, which demands that the soul dismiss any thought that is not directed to God. And in forgetfulness of all the things that are and happen in this short and miserable life.

(Counsels, 9)

Epistolary admonishments on prayer

21.

Along with these admonishments classified as anonymous, even though they were originally written to someone in particular, there are similar fragments among the few letters Saint John wrote in response to those seeking advice on their spiritual condition. In fact, the Saint's epistolary that has reached us is very brief, consisting of thirty letters in all. Yet, many deal explicitly with the topic of prayer. For instance, to a Carmelite nun who suffered from scruples he wrote the following:

Read, pray, rejoice in God, both your good and your salvation. May He grant you this good and this salvation and conserve it all until the day of eternity.

(Letters, 21)

22.

In the same letter he urges her to live the pentecostal period in close communion with the Spirit. In other words, his advice is to live everyday life in an attitude of prayer and contemplation without limiting prayer to a particular moment of the day.

In these days try to keep interiorly occupied with the desire for the coming of the Holy Spirit and on the feast and afterwards with His continual presence. Let your care and esteem for this be so great that nothing else will matter to you or receive your attention, whether it may concern some affliction or some other disturbing memories. And if there be faults in the house during these days, pass over them for love of the Holy Spirit and of what you owe to the peace and quietude of the soul in which He is pleased to dwell.

(Letters, 21)

23.

Certainly, there is no better teaching regarding our spiritual life and particularly prayer than the experience offered by the Saint in his letters, both to individuals in particular and to communities in their entirety.

In what concerns the soul, it is safest not to lean on anything nor desire anything. A soul should find its support wholly and entirely in its director, for not to do so would amount to no longer wanting a director. And when one director is not sufficient and suitable, all the others are useless or a hindrance. Let not the soul be attached to anything, for since prayer is not wanting, God will take care of His possessions; they belong to no other owner, nor should they.

(Letters, 10)

24.

I certainly believe it is a temptation the devil brings to your mind so that what should be employed in God is taken up with this. Be courageous, my daughter, and give yourself greatly to prayer, forgetting this thing and that, for after all we have no other good.

(Letters, 15)

25.

Take care of your soul and do not confess scruples or first motions or imaginings in which the soul does not desire to be detained. Look after your health and do not fail to pray when you can.

(*Letters*, 28)

26.

Our greatest need is to be silent before this great God with the appetite and with the tongue, for the only language He hears is the silent language of love.

(*Letters*, 7)

Commending ourselves to our neighbor's prayer

27.

Another significant detail that reveals Saint John's appreciation of prayer is the fact that in most of his letters he commended his particular needs to the prayers of his followers. In his letter to the Discalced nuns of Beas, he wrote:

I commend myself to your prayers; and be assured that although my charity is little, it is so directed toward you that I do not forget those whom I owe so much in the Lord.

(*Letters*, 7)

28.

Similarly, in other letters he wrote:

I have been somewhat ill. Now I am well, but Brother Juan Evangelista is sick. Commend him and me also to God, my daughter in the Lord.

(*Letters*, 19)

29.

What I ask you, daughter, are your prayers to the Lord that whatever happens He may continue to grant me this favor. I still fear they will make me go to Segovia.

(Letters, 23)

30.

Tell the same to Sister Juana, and commend me to God. May He be in your soul.

(Letters, 17)

31.

Give her my regards and commend me to God. Abide with Him. I cannot write at greater length.

(Letters, 13)

32.

In addition to commending himself to the prayer of others, the Saint promised to pray for their own needs. This proves his certainty of the efficacy and value of prayer as a spiritual aid.

They should all recommend to God, for I will never forget to do so for them.

(Letters, 34)

33.

I have not forgotten your business matter, but nothing more can be done now, although I have a great desire to do so. Entrust this earnestly to God and take our Lady and St. Joseph as your advocates in it.

(Letters, 11)

34.

Perhaps the best testimony of how much he treasured the prayer of others is found in the following letter to Doña Ana, in which he also conveys his congratulations to her brother Luis, a newly ordained priest. It is, moreover, a letter overflowing with deep affection.

Congratulate him for me. I dare not ask him that he might some day remember me at the sacrifice of the Mass, and I as a debtor will ever remember him. Even though I am forgetful, I will not be able to forget him, since he is so close to his sister whom I always remember. Greetings in the Lord to my daughter Doña Inés. And may both of you pray God to prepare me that He may bring me to Himself.

(Letters, 30)

REQUIREMENTS FOR MASTERING TRUE PRAYER

As we have seen before, rather than talking about the nature or pedagogy of prayer, Saint John of the Cross chose to delve into the requirements that constitute the cornerstone of authentic prayer, so that we do not believe we have that ability if those requirements are missing. In fact, in his prologue to the *Ascent of Mount Carmel* he warns us: "Likewise, many individuals think they are not praying, when, indeed, their prayer is intense. Others place high value on their prayer, while it is little more than nonexistent" (*Prologue, Ascent,* 6).

Saint John refers to two types of requirements that can contribute to lay an authentic foundation to our prayer. Some of these are internal, such as the disposition of our heart and our emotions, which we must use when resorting to prayer. Others are external such as the environment surrounding us when we pray. Still, even though the Saint talks about internal and external conditions, it may be more precise to say that only one condition really matters, that is our calling to live a relationship with God based upon our most radical and transparent faith, and our efforts to prevent ourselves from being excessively attached to superficial things, both internal such as our own preferences, and external, such as particular places, images, etc.

For the purpose of clarification we shall consider separately what the Saint says about two kinds of requirements, even if in many ways they happen to coincide.

1. Internal requirements

35.

Saint John believes that the central point of the internal require-
ments to lay the foundations of prayer is our "letting go"—the
spiritual nakedness required to encounter God. In other words,
our search should not be guided by the pleasure we may draw
from that encounter nor by our own wishes or personal preferen-
ces.

Cares are no molestation to the detached man, neither in prayer
nor outside of it, and thus, losing no time, he easily stores up an
abundance of spiritual good: yet the other spends all his time going
to and fro about the snare to which his heart is tied and attached,
and even with effort he can hardly free himself for a short while
from this snare of thought and joy over the object of his attached
heart.

(3 Ascent, 20:3)

36.

They are of the opinion that any kind of withdrawal from the
world or reformation of life suffices. Some are content with a certain
degree of virtue, perseverance in prayer, and mortification, but
never achieve the nakedness, poverty, selflessness, or spiritual
purity (which are all the same) that the Lord counsels us here.

(2 Ascent, 7:5)

a) Humbling ourselves completely and suffering for Christ

37.

I should like to persuade spiritual persons that the road leading
to God does not entail a multiplicity of considerations, methods,
manners, and experiences—though in their own way these may be
a requirement for beginners—but demands only the one thing necessary: true self-denial, exterior and interior, through surrender of self

both to suffering for Christ and to annihilation in all things. In the exercise of this self-denial everything else, and even more, is discovered and accomplished. If one fails in this exercise, the root and sum total of all the virtues, the other methods would amount to no more than going about in circles without any progress, even if they result in considerations and communications as lofty as those of the angels. A man makes progress only through the imitation of Christ, Who is the Way, the Truth, and the Life. No one goes to the Father but through Him, as He states Himself in St. John (Jn 14:6). Elsewhere He says: *I am the door, if any man enter by Me he shall be saved* (Jn 10:9). Accordingly, I should not consider any spirituality worthwhile that would walk in sweetness and ease and run from the imitation of Christ.

(2 Ascent, 7:8)

38.

Frequently spiritual persons use this refreshment of the senses under the pretext of prayer and devotion to God; and they so perform these exercises that we could call what they do recreation rather than prayer, and pleasing self rather than God. Though the intention of these persons is directed to God, the effect they receive is recreation of the senses, from which they obtain weakness and imperfection more than the quickening of their will and its surrender to God.

(3 Ascent, 24:4)

39.

To purge the will of its desires and vain joy in these objects, and direct it to God, you should strive in your prayer for a pure conscience, a will that is wholly with God, and a mind truly set upon Him. And, as I mentioned, you ought to choose the most withdrawn and solitary place possible, convert all your joy of will into the invocation and glorification of God.

(3 Ascent, 40:2)

b) Profiting by the pleasure we draw from meditation at the beginning of our journey

40.

Despite the need to be detached, Saint John cautiously points out that when starting out on our spiritual journey the pleasure we draw from meditation is not only legitimate but also convenient and serves as bait. He says:

For a better understanding of this beginners' stage, it should be known that the practice of beginners is to meditate and make acts and discursive reflection with the imagination. A person in this state should be given matter for meditation and discursive reflection, and he should by himself make interior acts and profit in spiritual things from the delight and satisfaction of the senses. For by being fed with the relish of spiritual things, the appetite is torn away from sensual things and weakened in regard to the things of the world.

But when the appetite has been fed somewhat, and has become in a certain fashion accustomed to spiritual things, and has acquired some fortitude and constancy, God begins to wean the soul, as they say, and place it in the state of contemplation. This occurs in some persons after a very short time, especially with religious, for in denying the things of the world more quickly, they accommodate their senses and appetites to God and, in their activity, pass on to the spirit which God works in them. This happens when the soul's discursive acts and meditations cease, as well as its initial sensible satisfaction and fervor, and it is unable to practice discursive meditation as before, or find any support for the senses. The sensory part is left in dryness because its riches are transferred to the spirit, which does not pertain to the senses.

(Flame, 32)

41.

According to Saint John's doctrine, meditation proper is a stage that should be lived with full consciousness. In other words, it should be considered a temporary stage to be superseded and not a permanent situation. In the Ascent, *he says:*

Those who imagine God through some of these figures (as an imposing fire or as brightness, or through any other forms) and think that He is somewhat like them are very far from Him. These considerations, forms, and methods of meditation are necessary to beginners that the soul may be enamored and fed through the senses, as we shall point out later. They are suitable as the remote means to union with God, which beginners must ordinarily use for the attainment of their goal and the abode of spiritual repose. Yet these means must not be so used that a person always employs them and never advances, for then he would never achieve his goal, which is unlike the remote means and unproportioned to it—just as none of the steps on a flight of stairs has any resemblance to the goal at the top toward which they are the means.

(2 Ascent, 12:5)

c) Paying attention to internal conversation

42.

The Saint also cautions us against our being led to a mis-interpretation of prayer. He believes the risk is even greater for those who have a sharper understanding, since they may take the simple effects of a natural discourse in their own mind to be a "revelation" from God. In this regard, he points out the following:

Yet some intellects are so lively and subtle that, while recollected in meditation, they reason naturally and easily about some concepts, and form locutions and propositions very vividly, and consequently think that these locutions are from God. But that notion is false, for an intellect, freed from the operation of the senses, has the capacity to do this and even more with its own natural light and without any other supernatural help. Such an occurrence is frequent. And many are deluded by it in thinking that theirs is the enjoyment of a high degree of prayer and communion with God; consequently they either write the words down themselves or have others do so. It comes about that the experience amounts to nothing, that no substantial virtue is derived from it, and that it serves for little more than inducing vainglory.

These people should learn to give importance to nothing other than sincere effort, the establishment of their wills in humble love, and suffering in imitation of the life and mortifications of the Son of God. This is the road to the attainment of every spiritual good, and not that other one of copious interior reasoning.

(2 Ascent, 29:8, 9)

43.

And he later adds:

When the locution originates from the vivacity and light of the intellect, the cause of everything is the intellect, and there is no accompanying activity of the virtues. The will can love naturally in the knowledge and light of those truths, yet after the meditation, it will remain dry. But the soul will have no inclination toward vanity unless the devil again tempts it about its experience.

(2 Ascent, 29:11)

44.

In the following paragraph taken from the Spiritual Canticle, *the Saint admirably explains that the additional requirement for prayer should be accompanied and supported by such things as our personal behavior and the prayers of others:*

For the attainment of God it is not enough to pray with the heart and the tongue and receive favors from others, but that together with this a soul must through its own efforts do everything possible. God usually esteems a work done by the individual himself more than many others done for him.

(Canticle, 3:2)

45.

And in the Flame *he equally states:*

As a result the Wise Man affirmed that the end of prayer is better than the beginning (Eccl 7:9), and it is commonly quoted that the short prayer penetrates the heavens. A person already disposed can make many and far more intense acts in a short time than someone undisposed can in a long time; and, by reason of his being so fully disposed, he usually remains for a long time in an act of love or contemplation.

(Flame, 1:33)

46.

However, in order to cast away any doubt as to what is most substantial and valuable to prayer in our spiritual lives, the Saint says in the Ascent:

For the sake of directing his joy in moral goods to God, the Christian should keep in mind that the value of his good works, fasts, alms, penances, etc., is not based upon their quantity and quality so much as upon the love of God practiced in them, and that consequently they are deeper in quality the purer and more entire the love of God is by which they are performed.

(3 Ascent, 27:5)

2. External requirements

After having drawn our attention to the intimate requirements of authentic prayer and especially the need our soul has of "letting go," the Saint, experienced in the usual obstacles met by the soul in its spiritual itinerary, dedicates a series of chapters at the end of the third book of the Ascent *to the dangers we may encounter when entertaining ourselves excessively or improperly with the external circumstances surrounding prayer. Once more, his advice constitutes an earnest invitation to search the most solid things and establish a dialogue and communication with God simply through faith.*

2.1 Devotional sites and objects

47.

Certainly, the Saint does not ban or invalidate the value of devotional sites or objects such as pictures or statues, which have always been considered commendable means of Christian piety by the Church. His intention is to warn us of the danger of converting those means into ends in themselves. In fact, our internal attachment to a particular place or image could make our prayer more apparent than authentic. Thus, regarding the objects of piety he says:

A person should be certain that the more he is attached with a possessive spirit to the image or motive, the less will his prayer and devotion ascend to God.

(3 Ascent, 35:6)

48.

Much could be said about the ignorance of many in their use of statues. Their foolishness reaches such a point that they trust more in one statue than in another and think that God will answer them more readily through it, even when both statues represent the same person, such as those of our Lord or our Blessed Lady. At the bottom of this idea is their greater attachment to the one work than to the other, which entails gross ignorance about communion with God and the cult and honor due Him Who looks only upon the faith and purity of the prayerful heart.

(3 Ascent, 36:1)

49.

And regarding the way to use said objects of piety without attaching our senses to them, he adds:

He should pay no attention to these accidents, dwell not upon the image but immediately raise his mind to what is represented. He should prayerfully and devotedly center the satisfaction and joy of his will in God or the saint being invoked, so that the painting and senses will not absorb what belongs to the spirit and the living person represented.

(3 Ascent, 37:2)

a) Miraculous images

50.

Saint John believes that if it is true that God bestows a larger amount of his love and power to one holy image rather than to another, and sometimes performs miracles through them in response to someone's prayer, then it is justifiable to resort to those images. He says in this regard:

God does not work miracles and grant favors by means of some statues in order that these statues may be held in higher esteem than others, but that through His wonderful works He may awaken the dormant devotion and affection of the faithful. Since, consequently, through the instrumentality of this statue, devotion is enkindled and prayer prolonged—both means by which God hears and grants one's petitions—God continues to bestow favors and work miracles because of the image, which in itself is no more than a painting, but He does so because of the faith and devotion that is had toward the saint represented.

(3 Ascent, 36:2)

51.

In addition to images, he refers specifically to the rosary:

One rosary is no more influential with God than another; His answer to the rosary prayer is not dependent upon the kind of rosary used. The prayer He hears is that of the simple and pure heart, which is concerned only about pleasing God and does not bother about the kind of rosary used, unless in regard to indulgences.

(3 Ascent, 35:7)

52.

Regarding the devotional sites, he resolutely says:

Many of them in their desire and gratification grow so attached to their oratory and its decoration that all their energy, which should be employed in prayer and interior recollection is expended on these things. They do not realize that, by not arranging their oratory in a way that would further interior recollection and peace of soul, they receive as much distraction as they would from other things; and at every step they become disquieted about this pleasure, and even more so if anyone wants to take it away from them.

(3 Ascent, 38:5)

53.

Even though it is better to pray in the place that is more respectable, one should in spite of this choose that place which least hinders the elevation of sense and spirit to God. This is the interpretation we should give to Christ's reply to the query of the Samaritan woman about the place best suited for prayer—the temple or the mountain. His answer was that true prayer is annexed neither to the temple nor to the mountain, but that the adorers who please the Father are those who adore Him in spirit and truth (Jn 4:20-24).

(3 Ascent, 39:2)

54.

Churches and quiet places are dedicated and suitable for prayer, for the church should be used for no other purpose. Nevertheless, in a matter of communion with God as interior as this, that place should be chosen which least occupies and attracts the senses. A spiritual person should not look for a spot pleasant and delightful to the senses, as some usually do, lest he become absorbed with the recreation, gratification, and delight of the senses rather than with God in spiritual recollection. A solitary and austere location is beneficial for the sure and direct ascent of the spirit to God without the impediment or detainment caused by visible things. Sometimes visible objects do aid in the elevation of the spirit, but this elevation is the result of immediately forgetting them in order to remain recollected in God. Our Saviour, to give us an example, chose for His prayer solitary places, those that were undistracting to the senses and raised the soul to God (such as the mountains that are elevated above the earth and usually barren of the objects that would provide sensitive recreation) (Mt 14:23).

(3 Ascent, 39:2)

b) Sites chosen by God

55.

In the same way he first discusses the value of some images he also refers to those places where God seems to have revealed himself more clearly, which would legitimize our resorting to them with more frequency. He says:

Yet it is good sometimes to return there for prayer, provided one's soul is divested of the desire for spiritual possessions. There are three reasons: first, it seems that although God is not bound to any place, He desires in granting the favor to receive praise there from that soul; second, the soul when there will be more mindful of thanking God for His favors; third, while remembering the graces received there, a more fervent devotion will be awakened.

(3 Ascent, 42:3)

56.

Why God chooses one place in which to receive praise more than another, He alone knows. What we should know is that He does all for our own benefit and so that He may hear our prayers in these places—or anywhere in which we beseech Him with integral faith. Yet there is much greater occasion to be heard in those places consecrated to His cult, since the Church has so marked and dedicated them.

(3 Ascent, 42:6)

57.

Later on, he summarizes this subject in the following words:

The truly spiritual person never considers nor becomes attached to the particular comfort of a place of prayer, for this would result from attachment to the senses. His interest is interior recollection in the forgetfulness of other things. He chooses the site that is freest of sensible objects and satisfactions and turns his attention from all these considerations so that unimpeded by any creature he may rejoice more in solitude with God. Some spiritual persons noticeably spend all their time in adorning oratories and making places agreeable to their own temperament or inclination and they pay little heed to interior recollection, which is the important factor. They are not very recollected, for if they were they would be unable to find satisfaction in these ways, but would grow tired of them.

(3 *Ascent*, 39:3)

58.

Moreover, Saint John warns us about the fact that some people may abandon prayer when those pleasures are no longer experienced:

With regard to the exterior harm, a person will be rendered incapable of praying everywhere, but will be able to pray only in those places suited to his taste, and thus be frequently wanting in prayer. As the saying runs, he knows no other book than that of his own village.

(3 *Ascent*, 41:1)

59.

He also adds:

The reason some spiritual persons never entirely enter into the true joys of spirit is a failure to renounce their desire for joy in these exterior and visible things. These persons should keep in mind that although the place dedicated and suited to prayer is the visible oratory or church and the motivating good is the image, these means

should not be so used that the satisfaction and delight of the soul
stems entirely from them, thereby causing one to forget to pray in
the living temple which is interior recollection of soul.

(3 Ascent, 40:1)

2.2 Our attachment to rites and ceremonies

60.

*Our attention is also drawn to another obstacle which could
impair the authenticity of our faith in resorting to prayer as well
as the efficacy of prayer. Saint John refers to our attachment to
certain rites and ceremonies:*

We shall prescind from those ceremonies which make use of
extravagant names or terms without meaning and other unsacred
things that ignorant, rude, and questionable persons usually inter-
mingle with their prayers, since these ceremonies are obviously evil
and sinful. And in many of them there is a secret pact with the devil
by which God is provoked to anger and not mercy.

(3 Ascent, 43:1)

61.

I want to speak only of those ceremonies used by many today
with indiscreet devotion, since these are not included in those other
suspect kinds. These people attribute so much efficacy to methods
of carrying out their devotions and prayers and so trust in them that
they believe that if one point is missing or certain limits have been
exceeded their prayer will be profitless and go unanswered. As a
result they put more trust in these methods than they do in the living
prayer, not without great disrespect and offense toward God.

(3 Ascent, 43:2)

62.

What is worse—and intolerable—is that some desire to experience
an effect in themselves: either the granting of their petition or the

knowledge that it will be granted at the end of those superstitious ceremonies. Such a desire would amount to nothing more than tempting God and would thereby seriously provoke His wrath. Sometimes God gives the devil permission to deceive them through an experience and knowledge of things far from profitable to their souls. They deserve this because of the possessiveness they bring into their prayer, by not willing what God wills but what they themselves will. Hence, because they do not put all their trust in God, nothing turns out well for them.

(3 Ascent, 43:3)

63.

The Saint's final answer is clear and convincing:

These individuals should know, then, that the more trust they put in these ceremonies the less confidence they have in God, and that they will not obtain from Him the object of their desire.

Some pray more for their own intention than for the honor of God. Although they pray with the supposition that if God is to be served their petition will be granted, and if otherwise, it will not, they nevertheless overmultiply their prayers for that intention because of their attachment to the object of their request and their vain joy in it. It would be better to convert these prayers into practices of greater importance, such as the purification of their consciences, and serious concentration upon matters pertinent to their salvation; and thus they ought to have far less regard for all these other petitions irrelevant to this. Through the attainment of more important goals, they will also obtain all that in this other intention is good for them, even though they do not ask for it. And they receive this answer to their prayer sooner and in a better way than if they had directed all their strength toward making the request.

(3 Ascent, 44:1)

2.3 Prayer of petition

64.

Determined to offer us practical advice so that our soul does not get entangled in different prayers without actually encountering God, the Saint refers to a special type of prayer which is certainly not the only but the most common, that is the prayer of petition. In fact, our resorting to God and to those who are close to us for help in our needs is a well-known recourse. We have already mentioned a few of the Saint's ideas on the subject in previous sections when referring to other conditions for attaining true prayer. Equally important are the following criteria:

To obtain an answer to the requests we bear in our hearts, there is no better means than to concentrate the strength of our prayer upon what is more pleasing to God. For then He will give us not only the salvation we beg for, but whatever else He sees is fit and good for us, even though we do not ask for it.

(*3 Ascent*, 44:2)

65.

In one's petitions, then, the energies of the will and its joy should be directed to God in the manner described. One should be distrustful of ceremonies unapproved by the Catholic Church; and the manner of saying Mass should be left to the priest, who represents the Church at the altar, for he has received directions from her as to how Mass should be said. And persons should not desire new methods as if they knew more than the Holy Spirit and His Church. If in such simplicity God does not hear them, let them be convinced that God will not answer them even if they invent more ceremonies. For God is such that if a person lives in harmony with Him and does His will, He will do whatever that person wants; but if the person seeks his own interests, it will be useless for him to speak to God.

(*3 Ascent*, 44:3)

66.

Every soul should know that even though God does not answer its prayer immediately, He will not on that account fail to answer it at the opportune time if it does not become discouraged and give up its prayer. He is, as David remarks, *a helper in opportune times and tribulations* (Ps 9:10).

(Canticle, 2:4)

67.

It is noteworthy that even though God has knowledge and understanding of all, and even sees the very thoughts of the soul, as Moses asserts (Dt 31:21), it is said, when He remedies our necessities, that he sees them and, when He answers our prayers, that He hears them. Not all needs and petitions reach the point at which God, in hearing, grants them. They must wait until in His eyes they arrive at the suitable time, season, and number.

(Canticle, 2:4)

68.

Some call the Bridegroom beloved, whereas He is not really their beloved because their heart is not wholly set on Him. As a result their petition is not of much value in His sight. They do not obtain their request until through perseverance in prayer they keep their spirit more continually with God, and their heart with its affectionate love more entirely set on Him. Nothing is obtained from God except by love.

(Canticle, 1:13)

69.

The discreet lover does not care to ask for what she lacks and desires, but only indicates this need that the Beloved may do what he pleases. When the Blessed Virgin spoke to her beloved Son at the wedding feast in Cana in Galilee, she did not ask directly for the wine, but merely remarked: *They have no wine* (Jn 2:3). And the sisters of Lazarus did not send to ask our Lord to cure their brother, but to tell Him that Lazarus whom He loved was sick (Jn 11:3). There are three reasons for this: first, the Lord knows what is suitable for us better than we do; second, the Beloved has more compassion when He beholds the need and resignation of a soul that loves Him; third, the soul is better safeguarded against self-love and possessiveness by indicating its lack, rather than asking for what in its opinion is wanting.

(Canticle, 2:8)

70.

A person will ask a soul in this state for prayers. The soul will not remember to carry out this request through any form of idea of that person remaining in the memory. If it is expedient to pray for him (that is, if God wants to receive prayer for this person), God will move its will and impart a desire to do so; at times God will give it a desire to pray for others whom it has never known nor heard of.

(3 Ascent, 2:10)

Praying as Christ prayed and taught us to pray

71.

Finally, the Saint urges all those who pray to make their prayer resemble Christ's, using the words he taught us in addressing the Father. His actual words have no waste:

And regarding other ceremonies in vocal prayers and other devotions, one should not become attached to any ceremonies or modes of prayer other than those Christ taught us. When His disciples asked Him to teach them to pray, Christ obviously, as one Who knew so well His Father's will, would have told them all that was necessary in order to obtain an answer from the Eternal Father; and, in fact, He only taught them those seven petitions of the *Pater Noster*, which include all our spiritual and temporal necessities, and He did not teach numerous other kinds of prayers and ceremonies (Lk 11:1-4). At another time, rather, He told them that in praying they should not desire much speaking because our heavenly Father clearly knows our needs (Mt 6:7-8). He only charged us with great insistence to persevere in prayer—that is, in the *Pater Noster*—teaching in another place that one should pray and never cease (Lk 18:1). He did not teach us a quantity of petitions but that these seven be repeated often, and with fervor and care. For in these, as I say, are embodied everything that is God's will and all that is fitting for us. Accordingly, when His Majesty had recourse three times to the Eternal Father, all three times He prayed with the same petition of the *Pater Noster*, as the Evangelists recount: *Father, if it cannot be but that I drink this chalice, may Your will be done* (Mt 26:39, 42; Mk 14:36; Lk 22:42).

And He taught us only two ceremonies for use in our prayers. Our prayer should be made either in the concealment of our secret chamber (where without noise and without telling anyone we can pray with a more perfect and pure heart), as He said: *When you pray enter into your secret chamber, and having closed the door, pray* (Mt 6:6); or if not in one's chamber, in the solitary wilderness, and at the best and most quiet time of night, as He did (Lk 6:12). No reason exists, hence, for designating fixed times or set days, or for choosing some days more than others for our devotions; neither is there reason for using other kinds of prayer, or phrases having a play on words, but only those prayers that the Church uses, and as she uses them, for all are reducible to the *Pater Noster*.

(*3 Ascent*, 44:4)

THE NIGHT AND THE STATE OF DRYNESS IN PRAYER

The Saint's doctrine on the "Night," the symbolism of which he studied in great depth, is undoubtedly the sharpest and most original contribution to his teaching as a whole. The "Night" means purification, detachment from all that is human to make union feasible. Thus, it is a necessary passage for those who walk toward God. Given the uniqueness of Saint John's doctrine on the subject, we shall quote in this chapter some of the things the Saint says in relation to the "Night" through which those who pray must transit. To justify the need for this purification, he describes in the first volume of *The Dark Night* the capital imperfections found in the beginner and naturally refers to his personal relationship with God in prayer.

72.

Regarding the beginner's zeal and exercise of prayer, he says:

The soul finds its joy, therefore, in spending lengthy periods at prayer, perhaps even entire nights.

(1 Night, 1:3)

Vices found in the beginner

73.

He then refers specifically to the beginner's imperfections and vices:

It will happen that while a soul is with God in deep spiritual prayer, it will on the other hand passively experience sensual rebellions, movements, and acts in the senses, not without its own great displeasure. This frequently happens at the time of Communion.

(1 Night, 4:2)

74.

Some people are so delicate that when gratification is received from the spirit or from prayer, they immediately experience a lust which so inebriates them and caresses their senses that they become as it were engulfed in the delight and satisfaction of that vice; and this experience will endure passively with the other.

(1 Night, 4:5)

75.

For when the delight and satisfaction procured in their spiritual exercises passes, these beginners are naturally left without any spiritual savor. And because of this distastefulness, they become peevish in the works they do and easily angered by the least thing, and occasionally they are so unbearable that nobody can put up with them. This frequently occurs after they have experienced in prayer some recollection pleasant to the senses. After the delight and satisfaction is gone, the sensory part of the soul is naturally left vapid and zestless, just as a child when withdrawn from the sweet breast.

(1 Night, 5:1)

76.

Once they do not find delight in this, or any other spiritual exercise, they feel extreme reluctance and repugnance in returning to it, and sometimes even give it up. For after all, as we mentioned, they are like children who are prompted to act not by reason but by pleasure.

All their time is spent looking for satisfaction and spiritual consolation; they can never read enough spiritual books, and one minute they are meditating upon one subject and the next upon another, always in search for some gratification in the things of God.

(1 Night, 6:6)

77.

Also regarding spiritual sloth, these beginners usually become weary in the more spiritual exercises and flee from them, since these exercises are contrary to sensory satisfaction. Since they are so used to finding delight in spiritual practices, they become bored when they do not find it. If they do not receive in prayer the satisfaction they crave—for after all it is fit that God withdraw this so as to try them—they do not want to return to it or at times they either give up prayer or go to it begrudgingly.

(1 Night, 7:2)

Dryness

78.

However, the "Night" encountered along the journey of prayer can be described more specifically as the experience of dryness. It is that distressing unwillingness that possesses our soul, rending every spiritual experience disagreeable, particularly prayer. Cost-

*ly as it may be to pay such a price in our everyday encounter with
God, it is even more painful when it becomes a lasting condition
we fear will never end. The Saint offers his advice with genuine
mastery.*

God does this after beginners have exercised themselves for a
time in the way of virtue and have persevered in meditation and
prayer. For it is through the delight and satisfaction they experience
in prayer that they have become detached from worldly things and
have gained some spiritual strength in God. This strength has helped
them somewhat to restrain their appetites for creatures, and
through it they will be able to suffer a little oppression and dryness
without turning back. Consequently, it is at the time they are going
about their spiritual exercises with delight and satisfaction, when
in their opinion the sun of divine favor is shining most brightly on
them, that God darkens the sun of light and closes the door and
spring of the sweet spiritual water they were tasting as often and
long as they desired . . . God now leaves them in such darkness that
they do not know which way to turn in their discursive imaginings;
they cannot advance a step in meditation, as they used to, now that
the interior sensory faculties are engulfed in this night. He leaves
them in such dryness that they not only fail to receive satisfaction
and pleasure from their spiritual exercises and works . . . but also
find these exercises distasteful and bitter. As I said, when God sees
that they have grown a little, He weans them from the sweet breast
so that they might be strengthened, lays aside their swaddling
bands, and puts them down from His arms that they may grow
accustomed to walking by themselves.

(1 Night, 8:3)

79.

Those who do not walk the road of contemplation act very
differently. This night of the aridity of the senses is not so continuous in them. . . .

For God does not bring to contemplation all those who purposely
exercise themselves in the way of the spirit, nor even half. Why? He
best knows.

(1 Night, 9:9)

80.

The attitude necessary in the night of sense is to pay no attention to discursive meditation, since this is not the time for it. They should allow the soul to remain in rest and quietude, even though it may seem very obvious to them that they are doing nothing and wasting time, and even though they think this disinclination to think about anything is due to their laxity. Through patience and perseverance in prayer, they will be doing a great deal without activity on their part. All that is required of them here is freedom of soul, that they liberate themselves from the impediment and fatigue of ideas and thoughts and care not about thinking and meditating. They must be content simply with a loving and peaceful attentiveness to God, and live without the concern, without the effort, and without the desire to taste or feel Him.

(1 Night, 10:4)

81.

Indeed, this is not the time to speak with God, but the time to put one's mouth in the dust, as Jeremiah says, that perhaps there might come some actual hope (Lam 3:29), and the time to suffer this purgation patiently. God it is who is working now in the soul, and for this reason the soul can do nothing. Consequently, a person can neither pray vocally nor be attentive to spiritual matters.

(2 Night, 8:1)

82.

The north wind is very cold, it dries up and withers the flowers and plants, or at least when striking them makes them shrink and close. Because the spiritual dryness and affective absence of the Beloved produces this same effect in the soul by extinguishing the satisfaction, delight, and fragrance of the virtues she was enjoying, she calls it a "deadening north wind." It deadens the virtues and affective exercise, and as a result the soul pleads, "Be still, deadening north wind."

It should be understood that this plea of the soul flows from prayer and the spiritual exercises and is directed toward a detainment of the dryness.

(Canticle, 17:3)

CONTEMPLATIVE PRAYER

Before setting out to compile Saint John's writings on prayer we drew the readers' attention to the fact that the Saint did not approach the subject of mental prayer thoroughly since it is a matter on which much was written and because he was addressing people who were already familiar with the topic. While the author makes frequent references to prayer, he offers more abundant doctrine on the topic of contemplation, which is a more elevated stage of prayer reached by a few privileged souls. However, we have already explained that the subject of contemplation exceeds the object of this book.

Nevertheless, the stage of contemplation can be reached by taking one step further in the journey of meditative prayer. Therefore, we should at least quote Saint John's references to the transition from one stage of prayer to another. Thus, we shall not demolish or wrongly interpret a given situation, preventing anyone from reaching the height of contemplation. According to Saint John, this danger is frequently faced not only by the fortunate soul called to contemplation but also by their spiritual advisors. The Saint refers to the latter both extensively and harshly in his comment to the third stanza of his poem *The Living Flame of Love*.

The drawbacks suffered by those who have an inadequate spiritual advisor

83.

Although this damage is beyond anything imaginable it is so common and frequent that scarcely any spiritual director will be found who does not cause it in souls God is beginning to recollect in this manner of contemplation. How often is God anointing a contemplative with some very delicate unguent of loving knowledge, serene, peaceful, solitary, and far withdrawn from the senses and what is imaginable, as a result of which this person cannot meditate, nor reflect on anything, nor enjoy anything heavenly or earthly (since God has engaged him in that lonely idleness and given him the inclination to solitude), when a spiritual director will happen along who, like a blacksmith, knows no more than how to hammer and pound with the faculties. Since hammering with the faculties is this director's only teaching, and he knows no more than how to meditate, he will say: "Come, now, lay aside these rest periods, which amount to idleness and a waste of time; take and meditate and make interior acts, for it is necessary that you do your part; this other method is the way of illusions and typical of fools."

(Flame, 3:43)

84.

These spiritual directors, not understanding souls that tread the path of quiet and solitary contemplation, since they themselves have not reached it and do not know what it is to part with discursive meditation, think these souls are idle. They hinder them and hamper the peace of restful and quiet contemplation, which God of His own was according them, by making them walk along the path of meditation and imaginative reflection and perform interior acts. In doing this, these souls find great repugnance, dryness, and distraction; they would want to remain in their holy idleness and quiet and peaceful recollection. Since the senses find nothing to be attached to, to take pleasure in, or do in this recollection, these directors also persuade souls to strive for satisfaction and feelings of fervor when they should be counseling the opposite. When these persons cannot accomplish this as before, because the time for such activity has passed and this is not their road, they grow doubly disquieted, thinking that they are lost. Their directors foster this belief in them, cause them aridity of spirit, and deprive them of the precious anointings God was bestowing on them in solitude and tranquillity. These directors do them serious harm, as I said, bringing them grief and ruin, for on the one hand such persons lose ground, and on the other hand they suffer a useless affliction.

(Flame, 3:53)

85.

For it is certain that since that soul must always advance along the spiritual road, on which God is always a help to it, it will have to change its style and mode of prayer and will need another doctrine more sublime than yours and another spirituality. Not everyone knows all the happenings and stages of the spiritual journey, nor is everyone spiritually so perfect as to know every state of the interior life in which a person must be conducted and guided. At least the director should not think that he has all the requirements, or that God will not want to lead the soul further on.

Not everyone capable of hewing the wood knows how to carve the statue.

(Flame, 3:57)

The harm the soul does to itself

86.

However, the spiritual advisor is not always the cause of the harm inflicted upon a soul. Each of us can be our own hindrance. In fact, the Saint says:

The third blind man is the soul which, by not understanding itself, disturbs and harms itself. Since it only knows how to act by means of the senses and discursive reflection, it thinks it is doing nothing when God introduces it into that emptiness and solitude where it is unable to use the faculties and make acts, and as a result it strains to perform these acts. The soul, therefore, that was enjoying the idleness of spiritual peace and silence, in which God was secretly adorning it, is distracted and filled with dryness and displeasure.

It will happen that while God persists in keeping the soul in that silent quietude, it persists in its desire to act through its own efforts with the intellect and the imagination. It resembles a child who kicks and cries in order to walk when his mother wants to carry him, and thus neither allows his mother to make any headway nor makes any himself; or it resembles one who moves a painting back and forth while the artist is at work so that either nothing is accomplished or the painting is damaged.

(Flame, 3:66)

Passively following the loving advice

87.

The writer explains the attitude that should be followed by those who find themselves in this predicament regarding meditation:

Hence a person at this time should be guided in a manner entirely contrary to the former. If, prior to this, directors suggested matter for meditation, and he meditated, now they should instead withhold this matter, and he should not meditate. For as I say, he is unable to do so even though he may want to, and were he to try he would be distracted instead of recollected . . . on the contrary he procures dryness . . . in losing the one good, he does not gain the other. . . .

Therefore directors should not impose meditation upon persons in this state, nor should they oblige them to make acts. . . . Thus the individual also should proceed only with a loving attention to God, without making specific acts. He should conduct himself passively, as we have said, without efforts of his own, but with the simple, loving awareness, as a person who opens his eyes with loving attention.

(Flame, 3:33)

88.

A person should not bear attachment to anything, neither to the practice of meditation, nor to any savor, whether sensory or spiritual, nor to any other apprehensions. He should be very free and annihilated regarding all things, because any thought would impede and disquiet him, and make noise in the profound silence of his senses and his spirit, which he possesses for the sake of this deep and delicate listening. God speaks to the heart in this solitude.

(Flame, 3:34)

89.

When it happens, therefore, that a person is conscious in this manner of being placed in solitude and in the state of listening, he should even forget the practice of loving attentiveness I mentioned so as to remain free for what the Lord then desires of him. He should make use of that loving awareness only when he does not feel himself placed in this solitude, or inner idleness or oblivion or spiritual listening.

(Flame, 3:35)

90.

This teaching also appears in the treatise of the Ascent of Mount Carmel, *in which the Saint offers similar practical advice. He dedicates chapter 14 of the second book to explain why the soul that reaches the threshold of contemplation can no longer meditate:*

Many spiritual persons, after having exercised themselves in approaching God through images, forms, and meditations suitable for beginners, err greatly if they do not determine, dare, or know how to detach themselves from these palpable methods. For God then wishes to lead them to more spiritual, interior, and invisible graces by removing the gratification derived from discursive meditation. They even attempt to hold on to these methods, desiring to travel the road of consideration and meditation, using images as before. They believe such procedure is a permanent requirement. They strive hard to meditate, but draw out little satisfaction, or none at all; rather their lot becomes aridity, fatigue, and restlessness of soul. This aridity augments as their striving through meditation for that former sweetness, now unobtainable, increases. A person will no longer taste that sensible food, as we said, but rather enjoy another food, more delicate, interior, and spiritual. He will not acquire this spiritual nourishment through the labor of his imagination, but by pacifying his soul, by leaving it to its more spiritual quiet and repose.

(2 Ascent, 12:6)

Why there is a stage in which our soul can no longer meditate

91.

First, because the person has been granted all the spiritual good obtainable through discursive meditation on the things of God. An indication of this is his inability to make discursive meditation as before, or derive from it the spirituality which was in store for him.

(2 Ascent, 14:1)

92.

The second reason is that he has now acquired the substantial and habitual spirit of meditation. It should be known that the purpose of discursive meditation on divine subjects is the acquisition of some knowledge and love of God. Each time a person through meditation procures some of this knowledge and love he does so by an act. Many acts, in no matter what area, will engender a habit. Similarly, the repetition of many particular acts of this loving knowledge becomes so continuous that a habit is formed in the soul. God, too, effects this habit in many souls, without the precedence of at least many of these acts as means, by placing them at once in contemplation.

(2 Ascent, 14:2)

93.

This is why a man experiences difficulty and displeasure when others, in spite of the calm he is enjoying, endeavor to force him to meditate and work with particular concepts. His experience resembles that of the suckling child which finds that the breast is taken away just when it is beginning to taste the milk that was gathered there for it, and as a result is forced to renew its efforts. Or like the experience of a man who, while enjoying the substance of the fruit, once the rind is peeled, is forced to stop and begin again to remove the rind from the fruit even though it has already been peeled. In such an instance he would fail to find the rind and cease to enjoy the substance of the fruit which he holds in his hands. Or this is like turning away from the captured prey to go hunting for another.

(2 Ascent, 14:3)

94.

Many behave similarly at the beginning of this state. They are of the opinion that the whole matter consists in understanding particular ideas and reasoning through images and forms (the rind of the spirit). Since they do not encounter these images in that loving, substantial quietude, where nothing is understood particularly and in which they like to rest, they believe they are wasting time and straying from the right road; and they turn back to search for the rind of images and reasoning. They are unsuccessful in their search because the rind has already been removed. There is no enjoyment of the substance nor ability to meditate, and they become disturbed with the thought of backsliding and going astray.

(2 Ascent, 14:4)

The enjoyment of loving tranquility is no time wasted

95.

The writer offers timely advice in order that we use this type of prayer more profitably.

Although, as we asserted, this prayer lasts a long while, it seems of brief duration to the individual, since he has been united with pure knowledge which is independent of time. This is the short prayer which, it is said, pierces the heavens (Eccl 35:21). It is short prayer because it is not subject to time, and it penetrates the heavens because the soul is united with heavenly knowledge.

(2 Ascent, 14:11)

96.

We did not mean that those beginning to have this general loving knowledge should never again try to meditate. In the beginning of this state the habit of contemplation is not so perfect that one can at will enter into this act, neither is one so remote from discursive meditation as to be always incapable of it. One can meditate naturally through forms and scenes as before, and discover something new in it. Indeed, at the outset, upon judging through the signs mentioned above that his soul is not occupied in repose and knowledge, a person will need to make use of meditation. This need will continue until he acquires the habit of contemplation in a certain perfect degree. The indication of this will be that every time he intends to meditate, he will immediately notice this knowledge and peace as well as his own lack of power or desire to meditate, as we said.

(2 Ascent, 15:1)

97.

When the spiritual person cannot meditate, he should learn to remain in God's presence with a loving attention and a tranquil intellect, even though he seems to himself to be idle. For little by little and very soon the divine calm and peace with a wondrous, sublime knowledge of God, enveloped in divine love, will be infused into his soul. He should not interfere with forms or discursive meditations and imaginings. Otherwise his soul will be disquieted and drawn out of its peaceful contentment to distaste and repugnance. And if, as we said, scruples about his inactivity arise, he should remember that pacification of soul (making it calm and peaceful, inactive and desireless) is no small accomplishment.

(2 Ascent, 15:5)

98.

In the Night, *the Saint also refers to this apparent loss of time:*

And even though more scruples come to the fore concerning the loss of time and the advantages of doing something else, since it cannot do anything or think of anything in prayer, the soul should endure them peacefully, as though going to prayer means remaining in ease and freedom of spirit. . . . If a model for the painting or retouching of a portrait should move because of a desire to do something, the artist would be unable to finish. . . .

(1 Night, 10:6)

99.

In regard to discursive meditation, in which an individual begins his quest for God, that it is true that he must not turn away from the breast of the senses for his nourishment until he arrives at the time and season suitable for so doing—that is, when God brings the soul to a more spiritual converse, to contemplation.

(2 Ascent, 17:7)

The right time to abandon meditation

100.

In chapter 13 of the second book of the Ascent *the Saint indicates three clear signals we should consider to judge whether or not it is the right time to abandon meditation:*

- one cannot make discursive meditation;
- awareness of a disinclination to fix the imagination or sense faculties upon other particular objects;
- a person likes to remain alone in loving awareness of God.

To leave safely the state of meditation and sense and enter that of contemplation and spirit, the spiritual person must observe within himself at least these three signs together.

(2 Ascent, 13-14)

101.

In his Spiritual Canticle *the writer also refers to the meditative prayer leading to contemplation and tells us how in this latter stage everything is transformed into a vital communication of love.*

It should be known that when the soul reaches this state, all the activity of the spiritual and sensory part (in what it does, or in what it suffers, and in whatever manner) always causes more love and delight in God, as we have said. Even the very exercise of prayer and communion with God, in which she was accustomed to considerations and methods, is now wholly the exercise of love. Hence whether her work is temporal or spiritual, this soul can always say, "Now that my every act is love."

(Canticle, 28:9)

The supreme value of love

102.

In his staunch and inflamed words, the Saint explains that this love should be the permanent driving force that consummates the union of our soul with God, at which point everything in our life and actions gains a more transcendental value. At the same time, he warns us to search and guard this love above everything else.

Let those, then, who are singularly active, who think they can win the world with their preaching and exterior works, observe here that they would profit the Church and please God much more, not to mention the good example they would give, were they to spend at least half of this time with God in prayer, even though they may not have reached a prayer as sublime as this. They would then certainly accomplish more and with less labor, by one work than they otherwise would by a thousand. For through their prayer they would merit this result, and themselves be spiritually strengthened. Without prayer, they would do a great deal of hammering but accomplish little, and sometimes nothing, and even at times cause harm.

God forbid that the salt should begin to lose its savor (Mt 5:13), for however much they may appear to achieve externally, they will in substance be accomplishing nothing; it is beyond doubt that good works can be performed only by the power of God.

(Canticle, 29:3)

103.

However, this state of union which is certainly the highest stage our soul may reach in this life is not equal to complete perfection. Thus, to prevent us from being shocked or scandalized the Saint warns us in the Ascent *that at this stage our soul may still harbor natural desires:*

It will even happen that while a person is experiencing an intense union of will in the prayer of quiet these appetites will be actually dwelling in his sensory part—yet the superior part of his soul will be paying no attention to them. But all the other voluntary appetites, whether they are the most serious, which involve mortal sin, or less grave in that they concern venial sin, or whether they be the least serious of all in that they only involve imperfections, must be mortified. A person must be liberated of them all, however slight they be, in order to arrive at this complete union.

(1 Ascent, 11:2)

This means that while we live in this world our union with God and consequently human perfection are both relative, which explains why both saints and mystics so often long for their definite encounter with God. However, while still waiting for that time to come, the soul must keep searching and growing in that union to achieve which it must resort to prayer as an instrument. Thus, we are in constant need of praying while we live as pilgrims in faith. Saint John taught us this last lesson not through his words but through his actions. He was, in fact, entranced in deep prayer while awaiting the arrival of death, hoping to resume his earthly prayer beyond death by singing his matins in heaven.
He died between two longings for prayer, the prayer lived throughout time and the prayer he dreamed of reciting for all eternity. In fact, his countless merits could only be crowned by that title that honors him forever: "Saint John, Master of Prayer."

SOURCES

John of the Cross did most of his writing during a relatively calm period of his life, between 1581 and 1588. It is safe to say that, apart from his letters, all his literary works were composed during his last fourteen years. Many of his original writings, unfortunately, have been lost, leaving copies, some of which appear to be only more or less faithful to what John actually wrote. Just the same, his poetry is considered among the finest and most important in Spanish literature, and the doctrine expressed in his works ranks him among the great spiritual teachers of all times. Today most people regard him as a master of mystical and ascetical theology, with both his poetry and prose offering solid guidelines on spiritual life.

Among the poems attributed to John of the Cross only ten are thought to be authentic, while four others are of questionable origin. The pieces of poetry chosen for this anthology reflect the profound personality of the Saint's prayers. They are from: *The Spiritual Canticle* (Spiritual Canticle); *I Live, but Not in Myself*; *The Dark Night* (Night); and *The Living Flame of Love* (Flame).

Besides poetry Saint John has four major prose works, all of which have been considered here in order to understand better his teaching on prayer. *The Ascent of Mount Carmel* (Ascent) and *The Dark Night* (Night) deal with the purification of the soul and the senses, while *The Spiritual Canticle* (Canticle) and *The Living Flame of Love* (Flame) are teachings addressed to Carmelites specifically on the topic of prayer. Along with these important commentaries he also wrote some minor works that consist mainly of observations and advise. Of these minor writings this work includes pieces from *Sayings of Light and Love* (Sayings), *Maxims on Love* (Maxims), *Counsels to a Religious on How to Reach Perfection* (Counsels), and *Degrees of Perfection* (Degrees). Reference is likewise made to selections from his correspondence (Letters). There are only thirty letters of the many he wrote that are still in existence, some addressed to individuals, while others to entire communities. His letters offer a very clear indication of his thought on prayer and highlight how central he considered it to everyday life.

Also included in this anthology is a report written by one of the Saint's religious brothers, Eliseo dei Martiri. Eliseo lived with John for a relatively long period of time and after John's death was asked to write a report about his memories of John of the Cross' ideas and sayings. The resulting document is called *Spiritual Suggestions* (Suggestions); it gives a helpful view, for our purposes, of John's method of prayer.

Throughout the text of this anthology the mood changes between prose and poetry to properly reflect each theme on prayer. Although Saint John's titles of both prose and poetry are at times the same, the poetic layout of the text and the brief introductions between each piece should adequately distinguish the two.

All translations, excluding those from *Spiritual Suggestions,* which are translated directly from the original Spanish, are from *The Collected Works of St. John of the Cross* (Washington, D.C.: ICS Publications, 1979), translated by Kieran Kavanaugh, O.C.D. and Otilio Rodrigues, O.C.D. These are used with permission from the publisher.

CHRONOLOGY

1542   June 24. Juan de Yepes y Alvarez is born in Fontiveros, Spain. He is named after St. John the Baptist.

1563   After having completed four years of formation in humanities at a Jesuit college, John enters the Carmelite Order at the monastery of Santa Anna in Medina del Campo.

        February 24. John receives the habit of Our Lady of Mount Carmel and changes his name to Juan de Santo Matía.

1564   For the next four years John studies art and theology at the University of Salamanca. He does most of his theological studies, though, at the College of San Andrés.

1567   John is ordained a priest during the Spring but celebrates his first mass only in early September in his home town, Medina del Campo. Here he meets Teresa of Avila for the first time and decides to follow her in her renewal of the Carmelite Order.

1568   Having finished his studies in theology John becomes more familiar with Teresa and her work. She arranges for him and two others to start in Duruelo the first community of men who follow the Reform. He changes his name to Juan de la Cruz (John of the Cross).

1570   In June the small but growing community moves to Mancera de Abajo. Not much later Teresa founds a house of studies in Alcalá; John is appointed rector.

1572   Upon the request of Teresa, John becomes vicar and confessor at the Convent of the Incarnation where she is prioress.

1576 John is removed from his position at Incarnation by order of the Calced Carmelites, only to be then restored to it by Spain's Papal Nuncio, Nicolás Ormaneto.

1577 December 3. The Calced Carmelites declare John a rebel and imprison him.

1578 August 17-18. After much suffering and hardship John escapes from his prison cell and heads for the south of Spain. During a Discalced Carmelite Chapter in October, John is elected prior of the monastery of El Calvario. The new Papal Nuncio, Felipe Sega, declares this Chapter null and void and excommunicates all participants, John included. Not hearing this news, John takes over his new position at El Calvario.

1579 John is assigned the task of founding a college in southern Spain in order to educate the students of the Reform. He becomes its rector.

1580–1590 The Discalced Carmelites are finally given juridical independence. John devotes his time to the work of the Reform, holding many important positions in the Order. He does much of his writing during this period.

1591 Due to a disagreement within the Order, for the first time John is not elected to any office. He is sent to Andalusia, joyfully relieved of all responsibility. Shortly afterward a process is begun to expel John from the Reform. In the meantime he becomes ill and moves to Ubeda, because there, he says, "nobody knows me."

 December 13. John dies at the age of 49. He receives the favor he had asked God for earlier: not to die a superior; to die in a place where he is unknown; and to die after having suffered much.

1675 John is beatified.

1726 John is canonized a Saint.

1926 John is declared a Doctor of the Catholic Church.